Victori[a] Pla[ys]

C000279582

Talent, Good Fun, Pat and Margaret

'Pigeon-holers will find a space for her beside Joe Orton and Ken Dodd . . . but her voice is characteristically and aggressively female. Just like *Talent* the play with songs which won her a couple of "most promising playwright" awards, *Good Fun*'s rude words, hilarious gags and the insights which are more varied than either are all in the mouths of the women at its centre.' *New Statesman*

'*Good Fun* is a sour but very funny comedy by Victoria Wood, who also acts in it and sings some of the songs. She is an ingenious lyricist, satirist and an engaging performer. The conception of this anti-musical is monstrous and daring – it concludes with 300 cystitis sufferers turning up at a party for which preparations have not been made.' James Fenton, *Sunday Times*

Talent: 'The first and last thing to be said about *Talent* is that it is very funny – at times, too near the knicker-wetting degree. Set backstage at a northern club's talent nite . . . in its short and pithy span it incorporates a wealth of human disillusion and more comic one-liners than is altogether fair in a sad, sad story.' *Guardian*

'*Pat and Margaret* is the most impressive thing that Wood has written. She displays an Orton-esque grasp of the grotesque in being able to explore trauma and tension, but with a touch so light that what would otherwise have been unbearably monstrous becomes mirthful.' *Time Out*
'Victoria Wood on top form.' *Observer*

Victoria Wood was born in Prestwich, Lancashire, in 1953. She is one of Britain's top comedians and the only one ever to have sold out fifteen consecutive nights at the Royal Albert Hall. Her first stage play, *Talent* (1978), was awarded the *Plays and Players* and *Evening Standard* Award for Most Promising Playwright. It was then adapted for television in 1979 and won the Pye Television Most Promising New Writer Award. Victoria susbsequently wrote two television plays, *Nearly a Happy Ending* and *Happy Since I Met You*, and a second stage play, *Good Fun* (Sheffield Crucible 1980; King's Head Theatre, London, 1981). Her television series include *Wood and Walters* and the two *As Seen on TV* series, followed by a TV special which won BAFTA awards for Best Light Entertainment Programme in 1986 and 1987. She has performed a series of one-woman shows in theatres all over Britain, including the London Palladium in 1987. Her previous books, *Lucky Bag: The Victoria Wood Song Book*; *Up To You, Porky: The Victoria Wood Sketch Book*; and *Barmy: The New Victoria Wood Song Book* were based on these shows. Her first full-length comedy film, *Pat and Margaret*, was screened by the BBC in September 1994.

VICTORIA WOOD

Plays: 1

Talent
Good Fun
Pat and Margaret

introduced by the author

Methuen Drama

METHUEN DRAMA CONTEMPORARY DRAMATISTS

This edition first published in Great Britain in 1998
by Methuen Drama

Good Fun and *Talent* first published in Great Britain
in a volume together in 1988 by Methuen London
Copyright © 1988 by Victoria Wood
Pat and Margaret first published in Great Britain in 1994
by Methuen London
Copyright © 1994 by Victoria Wood
Collection and Introduction copyright © 1998 by Victoria Wood

The author has asserted her moral rights

A CIP catalogue record for this book is available at the British Library.

ISBN 0 413 72970 2

Typeset by Deltatype Ltd, Birkenhead, Merseyside
Transferred to digital printing 2002.

Contents

Chronology   vii

Introduction   ix

TALENT   1

GOOD FUN   51

PAT AND MARGARET   131

Victoria Wood
A Chronology

1974	Won ATV's *New Faces*
1975	*The Summer Show*, ATV sketch show with Marti Caine and Lenny Henry
	Played Edinburgh Festival and Hampstead Theatre with *G.R.I.M.M.S*, a revue with Roger McGough
	Sang on *That's Life* with Esther Rantzen
1977–82	*Funny Turns*, a revue with husband, Geoffrey Durham, magician
1978	Performer/contributor to *In at the Death*, a revue at the Bush Theatre, London, with Julie Walters
	Talent premiered at the Crucible Theatre, Sheffield. Won the *Plays and Players* Award and the *Evening Standard* Award for the Most Promising Playwright
1979	*Talent* adapted for television, starring Victoria Wood and Julie Walters. Won Pye Television Award for Most Promising Writer
1980	*Nearly a Happy Ending*, a play for Granada Television
	Good Fun, a musical, opened at the Crucible Theatre, Sheffield
1981	*Happy Since I Met You*, a play for Granada Television
	Wood and Walters, comedy series for Granada Television
1982	*Funny Turns*, West End season at the Duchess Theatre, London
1983–4	Toured with *Lucky Bag*, the first of her six solo stand-up shows
1985	*Victoria Wood – As Seen On TV*, television comedy series for BBC 2. Won Broadcasting Press Award, BAFTA Best Light Entertainment Programme and Best Light Entertainment Performance
	Lucky Bag: The Victoria Wood Song Book published
1986	*Victoria Wood – As Seen On TV*, second series.

	Won BAFTA Best Light Entertainment Programme
	Up To You, Porky published
1987	*Victoria Wood On TV – Special.* Won BAFTA Best Light Entertainment Programme
	Won BBC Personality of the Year from the Variety Club of Great Britain
	Barmy published
	Sell-out run of solo stand-up at the London Palladium
1988	*An Audience with Victoria Wood* for London Weekend Television. Won BAFTA Best Light Entertainment Programme and Best Light Entertainment Performance
1989	*Victoria Wood*, six half-hour plays for the BBC
1990	*Mens Sana in Thingummy Doodah* published
	Visited Ethiopia for Comic Relief to make a documentary, *Money Well Spent*
	Victoria Wood Up West, new show at the Strand Theatre, London, for ten weeks followed by tour
1992	*Victoria Wood's All Day Breakfast*, Christmas Day Special for BBC1
1993	Tour culminating in fifteen-night sell-out run at the Royal Albert Hall
1994	*Pat and Margaret*, screenplay, co-starring with Julie Walters. Won Broadcasting Press Guild Award for Best Single Drama
	Recorded Christmas TV Special based on stage show
1995	Travelled to Zimbabwe for Comic Relief to stay with a family of farmers – filmed for Red Nose Day
	Recorded one episode of *Great Railway Journeys of the World*
1996	New show culminating in another fifteen-night sell-out run at the Royal Albert Hall
	South Bank Show documentary with Melvyn Bragg about Victoria Wood on tour
	Chunky published
1997	Recorded show *Victoria Wood Live 1997*, for video release
	Awarded OBE
	Toured Australia and New Zealand
1998	*dinnerladies*, six-part sit-com for the BBC

Introduction

I wrote *Talent* in 1978. That summer, I appeared in a revue called *In at the Death* at the Bush Theatre in London. I met a director, David Leland and he suggested that I and one of the co-authors of the revue, Ron Hutchinson, should collaborate on a play about strippers for the 1978 New Play Season at the Crucible Theatre, Sheffield.

The Bush Theatre was over a pub which had strippers and Ron and I spent twenty minutes one evening watching a large girl in boots walk out of the ladies' lavatory, take off her clothes (she kept on her boots, the floor was filthy) and walk back into the ladies' lavatory again.

Then Ron said he was too busy to do this play, and David asked me if I would do it on my own. Not knowing anything about the world of the stripper and having all the investigative zeal of a defrosting beefburger, I decided to try and think up an idea of my own. The idea came quite easily, though typing it out was quite difficult.

I had always been fascinated by talent contests and had entered quite a few in my late teens and early twenties. I never won, though in a Birmingham nightclub I once came third on the clapometer. I found out a few years later there had never been a clapometer, it was a vanity case with some paper round. I was also interested in the relationship between attractive sparky girls and big fat plain ones.

The play was produced that autumn in Sheffield, directed by David Leland and I played Maureen. I had never intended to appear in the play at all, though everyone assumed I had written it with the express purpose of drinking Babycham and having my bosoms fondled nightly. Because I was playing the piano in the show as well, it made the songs much easier to stage and I think that worked better than having a band. I have never seen it done since in the way that we did it, I suppose because fat actresses who can double as musical director are thin on the ground (or fat on the ground).

There was talk of a West End transfer but the running-time was one hour twenty minutes which was not considered a commercial length at that time. We did pop into the ICA with it, which I didn't enjoy so much because there was no dartboard and the dressing-rooms were freezing. The set was a filthy old carpet covered in fag ends, which presented an irresistible challenge to the ICA cleaner. In the end we had to prop up a notice in Polish (not polish, you can't read it so well) saying 'Please don't hoover this carpet'.

The following year, Michael Codron, who had liked *Talent*, commissioned me to write another play. I wrote one called *Pals* which he said was 'very enjoyable'. This is a euphemism for wincing, so it went in the bin. I then wrote another one called *Good Fun*, which was produced at the Crucible, directed by David Leland in 1980. There was an awful lot wrong with it but there were some lovely performances and the audiences enjoyed it. The plan then was to re-write it and do it a couple of months later, again at the Crucible and perhaps transfer to the West End. I changed it, trying to lose the boring bits and put in a lot of Plot. I thought you had to have Plot in plays and so you do, but it helps if there's a good reason for it. The second time around it had more excellent performances and it went down extremely well with the audience but I didn't really know what I was doing with it and never got it right. Because I was playing Elsie, I never had the chance to sit outside and look at the play objectively and I think that would have helped. I watched another production of it at the King's Head Theatre in Islington and at the interval I heard a man say 'It's a bit witty witty, isn't it?'

After *Good Fun* I concentrated on television comedy and establishing myself as a stand-up comic. I also wrote two stage plays, which to save bothering Michael Codron, I called 'very enjoyable' and put straight in the bin.

If anybody is thinking of performing either *Talent* or *Good Fun*, here are some helpful tips.

1. In *Talent*, go easy on the Babycham. It makes you burp, which can ruin a girl's timing.

2. There is a lot of smoking in both plays. Be careful, this can damage your health and set fire to the costumes.

3. Elsie in *Good Fun* is not really a part at all. It is some jokes and an anorak. When the play overran originally, I cut my

lines first to avoid ill-feeling. Just keep smiling and shouting, is my advice.

Fast forward to 1991, when I had the idea for two estranged sisters re-united on a *Surprise Surprise*-type television programme. Originally conceived as a feature film, it was dropped by the company who bought it, so I bought it back and the BBC did it in 1994 as a Screen One. It was directed beautifully I thought, by Gavin Millar, and when I think of the small-scale British films that became big hits in the three or four years following, I do wonder how it would have fared as a feature. But I was terribly pleased with how it turned out, and really enjoyed just playing Margaret, after two years' heavy touring with a stand-up show.

I was interested in fame and celebrity, in the clash that comes when someone who believes their own publicity is forced to confront their past and their real family. I was also interested in exploring the life of someone like Margaret, who by force of circumstance, is never able to move very far from the world into which she was born. I wanted to explore what happened when a seemingly content and kind person like her was brought up against a sister whose life was on the surface more materially comfortable and enjoyable.

I suppose I had reached that age, I was about forty, when I had started to look back at my own youth, in Bury, near Manchester, and think about the changes that had happened to me since I had become a television performer, and how easy celebrity makes it to distance oneself from the pre-famous self. Also it was a good chance to put a funny wig on and fry chips.

A few weeks ago, I went to see *Talent* on tour, done as a period piece, with an actress playing Maureen who looked not unlike I had done twenty years before. As the play unfolded, what came into my mind, was not previous productions, but the little flat in Morecambe where I had written that first play, in three weeks of working through the night, leaving the pages out in the morning for my boyfriend to type. When *Talent* was shown on television and there was a lot of press attention, an article came out in the *TV Times*, saying I lived next door to a boarding house with sauce bottles in the window. The landlady, the aptly named Mona, was furious and refused to believe I hadn't written the piece myself to show her up. It was then I started to see there might be a few disadvantages to being famous.

Victoria Wood
1998

Talent

Talent was first performed at the Crucible Theatre Studio, Sheffield, in September 1978 with the following cast:

JULIE, *secretary, 24,*	Hazel Clyne
MAUREEN, *typist, 25,*	Victoria Wood
GEORGE FINDLEY, *retired factory worker, 69,*	Roger Sloman
ARTHUR HALL, *factory worker, 59,*	Bill Stewart
MEL, *junior sales executive, 31,*	Eric Richard
COMPERE, *assistant manager of a cabaret club, 44,*	Peter Ellis

Directed by David Leland

Talent subsequently transferred to the ICA, London in February 1979 with the following cast changes:

ARTHUR HALL	David Ellison
COMPERE	Jim Broadbent

Set

A small room behind the stage of a cabaret club. Two doors — one leading to the stage and one opening onto a corridor. It is full of discarded furniture: chairs, cupboards, a table with a mirror propped up on it, a filing cabinet, guitar and drum cases piled in a corner. A few coats hanging near them. Old beer cans and full ashtrays. No curtains. Outside the room is a corridor with a pay phone near the door.

In a separate area, but in full view of the audience, is a piano.

Lights up on the piano area.

JULIE, *accompanied by* MAUREEN, *sings 'JULIE' in her best club-singer voice:*

Julie

Julie — on a rainy day,
You're the girl that sings the clouds away,
One ray of that special kind of sunshine all your own.
Julie — on a snowy street,
Shining through the cold and driving sleet,
Your heat, just one smile can melt a frozen heart of stone.
It's true, I think you always knew,
There was something you should do,
Turn the key,
You'll be what you want to be, Julie.

Julie was a special child,
Maybe you would think was kind of wild,
Till she smiled, then you knew she was no ordinary girl.
Julie — with the lucky face,
In a pack of cards she would always find the ace,
In an oyster she would always find the pearl.
At school, always played the fool,
Broke every single rule,
But she,
Saw what no one else could see, Julie.

Julie — time is moving on,
Take your opportunity before it's gone,
You're one in a million, there is no one else like you.
Julie — it's your solo dance,

Life is knocking, will you take your chance,
Advance to the summit of the world and see the view.
More — there's even more in store,
Open up the door,
Turn the key,
You'll be what you want to be, Julie.

At the end of the song, lights go out on the piano, and come up on the room.

JULIE comes into the room, carrying a small vanity-case, and the sheet music of Cabaret. *She puts down her vanity-case on the table with the mirror on it, pulls up the strongest chair, admires the effect. Looks round, goes to the door, opens it, calls:*

JULIE. Maureen! I'm in here — come on.

> *MAUREEN comes in, carrying two handbags, a large vanity-case, a long dress on a hanger and a pair of shoes.*

> Where've you been, you were right behind me a minute ago.

MAUREEN. The man said the third door on the right.

JULIE. I know.

MAUREEN. I went in the third door on the right and it was full of gas meters and toilet paper.

JULIE. You might have known that wasn't a real door — it's only about two-foot high. That's where the dwarves get changed, the real people come in here.

MAUREEN. Well, where shall I put these things?

JULIE. Just put them down and shut the door, someone might come.

> *MAUREEN does so. JULIE begins to take all her make-up out and line it up on the table.*

MAUREEN. I didn't think it'd be like this, did you?

JULIE. Why?

MAUREEN. Well, when I won the colouring competition in the *Evening News*, I was invited backstage to meet Harry Secombe at the Palace Theatre as part of the prize. 'Sleepytime Elves' I had to colour in and I remember having terrible trouble with the stripes on their pyjamas. Course that was before felt tips . . .

JULIE. Well, we went to see Freddie Garrity once, you know, Freddie and the Dreamers, in his dressing-room and that was like somebody's sitting-room. It had a telly and a bed and everything. I went off him though 'cos he had a string vest. Our Viv threw an apple core at him.

MAUREEN. What for?

JULIE. For a laugh. She was right mad then. She used to wear one green sock and one red one. She's been all right since she got married.

MAUREEN. It's not very nice here is it?

JULIE. It doesn't matter — I've got to start somewhere. It'll be better in the finals. Ey, what time is it? Give us a fag.

MAUREEN. Twenty five to.

JULIE. God is that all. There's ages yet. I'd better start though just in case. What time is it?

MAUREEN. Twenty-five to.

JULIE. Oh yeah. (*Combing hair.*) Were you waiting ages for me? I was cheering our goldfish up and I put my hand in to stroke it and I still had my watch on. My mother tried to make me bring their alarm clock but I said I don't want anyone mistaking me for a bomb scare. And then I had that funny bus conductor, he's got a quite nice body but cross-eyes, he has this thing, he always pretends he's not going to let me off the bus.

MAUREEN. I never have any trouble with him.

JULIE. God, I'm nervous. I couldn't sleep last night. I was reading our Mark's *Beano* at 4 o'clock this morning. Then, I thought, I might as well sit in the garden and watch the sun come up.

MAUREEN. What was that like?

JULIE. It didn't bloody come up. I thought it must be behind the brickworks so I got the stepladder out, and climbed up.

Then I thought this is a bit stupid, standing out here in my rollers, so I went in and had my breakfast. Chocolate spread butties and liver sausage.

MAUREEN. That's very nutritionally unbalanced.

JULIE. I'm like that me — daring. It's no wonder I've got these bags under my eyes, staying awake all night. Shall I put my face pack on?

MAUREEN. Now? In here?

JULIE. Hey listen. 'Contains extracts of honey, cucumber and wild strawberries to soothe and tone the skin, witch-hazel and lavender to close the pores.' (*In Larry Grayson voice*:) Shut that pore!

MAUREEN. You better not put it on now, someone might come.

JULIE *starts to cleanse her face, then tones, moisturises, then makes-up.*

JULIE. I'll leave it in case I feel hungry later. God my hands are shaking you know. I haven't been so keyed up about anything since I was the Virgin Mary.

MAUREEN. That's going back a bit.

JULIE. You're not kidding. That compère's nice isn't he? He was at the audition. He said 'hallo' to me when I came in, did you see? He said 'Hallo Julie, it's the little girl with the big voice.' Give's another fag. Hey, I hope I don't lose my voice. I've had a real bad throat this week. And I was practising half the night last night. (*Clears throat — sings*:) 'Take the ribbon from your hair . . . ' Do I sound all right?

MAUREEN. Mm, OK.

JULIE. I think I sound really croaky. I bumped into Janice Harper outside Lewis's and she thought I sounded really croaky.

MAUREEN. Sounds all right to me.

JULIE. You wouldn't know. You're not exactly a bat, are you, when it comes to hearing?

MAUREEN. What do you mean a bat?

JULIE. Honestly, this morning, Mr Brennand was stood behind you for ages before you turned round. He said never mind collecting for Christine's wedding present, we all ought to be giving for a hearing-aid for you.

MAUREEN. I told you, I had cotton wool in my ears, I do sit practically two inches away from a pneumatic drill you know. I'm just about up the wall with it, it's been going on for weeks. My father says you never will get tarmac laid quickly under a Labour Government.

JULIE. That one with the curly hair asked me out the other day.

MAUREEN. What did you say?

JULIE. Well you can't when you're engaged, can you? Hey, what time is it?

MAUREEN. Quarter to.

JULIE. God there's still ages yet. Do you think blue mascara's out?

MAUREEN. Not if you've got blue eyes.

JULIE. No, I think I read it was out anyway, and only to use black. Fibres are out as well. Oh, bloody hell.

MAUREEN. What's the matter?

JULIE. 'Coats your lashes with fibres.' Damn. Oh well, it'll have to do. Is there a paper bag in my handbag with tights in?

MAUREEN. Yes.

JULIE. My Mum's made me bring clean knickers. I said no one'll know unless I make an announcement, but I don't like arguing with her since her operation.

MAUREEN. Is she better now?

JULIE. Well she can't wear stretch-pants and she's not to move the spin-drier for a few weeks but she's OK. They've all had it done in our street.

MAUREEN. What?

JULIE. Having your insides out. What my Nan would call your

'doings.' Mind you, once that's out you've had it. Or rather you don't have it, because I don't think you bother with it much after that. The man next door says it's like waving a Woody in the Albert Hall. I don't know how we got onto that — I only went round to borrow his secateurs.

MAUREEN. What's a Woody?

JULIE. Woodbine. He's obsessed, that man. He has all sorts of dirty magazines. Our Mark's the paper boy and he always has a quick flip through in the cemetery before he delivers them. I don't know what I'm on about — I went to Zena's to borrow her underskirt, and she had a whole crate of Babychams — we had loads.

MAUREEN. What was she doing with a crate of Babychams?

JULIE. Her Dad gets them — he works in a garage. She had two hundred and eighty Kit-Kats once.

MAUREEN. That's not bad.

JULIE *gets an underskirt out of the large vanity-case and holds it up against herself.*

JULIE. That's more your sort of thing isn't it, chocolate? Honestly, I'll never forget you at our house that Christmas Eve. 'Let's start the second layer in the Black Magic,' my Dad says, and there's just a lot of black crinkly paper and you with a red face.

MAUREEN. I brought them.

JULIE (*fingering minute roll of fat round her waist*). Look at that — I'm getting really fat. They'll have to push me round on wheels soon. I think I'm going on a diet — you ought to go on it with me. You could get some decent clothes then.

MAUREEN. It's glands.

JULIE. Well you shouldn't eat so many. You ought to be able to lose some of it anyway. How much do you weigh?

MAUREEN. I don't know. About — 10½. I've got very big bones. Angus likes me as I am anyway.

JULIE. He doesn't know how you are. He's in Australia.

MAUREEN. New Zealand. I send photographs.

JULIE. You mean you go in a booth on the station with a scarf on and your cheeks sucked in. When's he coming back?

MAUREEN. He gets three weeks in 1981.

JULIE. Here, look in that vanity-case. Zena gave me some Babychams, do you want one? Oh, you don't drink, do you?

MAUREEN. I do, I had two lager and limes at lunchtime actually. (*She opens two Babycham bottles.*) Where's the glasses?

JULIE. Don't be so soft Maur, drink it out the bottle.

MAUREEN *sings 'I Don't Know Why I'm Here':*

I Don't Know Why I'm Here

I don't know why I'm here — it's not much fun,
There's lots of other things I might have done,
Played Monopoly I might have won,
I usually do.
My father's banker — does it very well.
He's not really one, you couldn't tell.
Our Cindy weed on Mayfair and swallowed a hotel
And nearly choked to death.

We play Mastermind, I feel a fool,
I get the answers wrong, it's just like school.
We have an egg-timer, a torch and the piano stool,
We have to say our names.
Or sometimes Mrs Finch, the lady next door,
Comes round with her slides of the Second World War.
They're very amusing, I've seen them all before,
But you can't say that, can you?

We have home-made wine, it's very nice with Coke,
Father says 'Oh, Chateau Boots' and pretends to choke,
'From the south side of the shopping precinct,' it's just a joke,
It sounds funny when he says it.

At the end of a perfect day,
I kneel by my bed and pray
That the morning will find me changed
And no one will think it strange,

They'll just like me, or love me . . .
I don't know what to say
It won't happen anyway
Forget I said anything
I know what the day will bring
The same as yesterday

JULIE. Hey, I'm dying to go to the loo. I'm always like this when I'm excited — go and ask someone where it is eh?

MAUREEN. I'm not your servant you know.

JULIE. Go on Maur — I can't get my sockets right if I don't do them both at the same time.

MAUREEN. I can't go and ask someone where the toilet is . . .

JULIE. Why not?

MAUREEN. Well, who shall I ask? There isn't anybody here I don't think.

JULIE. Go and have a look round then. Hurry up Maur, I can't wait much longer.

MAUREEN *leaves.* JULIE *carries on with her eye make-up.* MAUREEN *comes back in.*

Did you find one?

MAUREEN. Yes . . . There's no lock . . .

JULIE. That doesn't bother me. I'm quite good at doing all that stuff. (*Mimes sitting down, leaning forward to hold the door shut.*) My sister did that once, and someone burst in and broke her wrist. Where is it?

MAUREEN. It doesn't flush.

JULIE. Is it really bad?

MAUREEN. It's like the ones in the park — near the drinking fountain.

JULIE. I'm definitely not going then. (*Showing closed eyelids to* MAUREEN:) Do you like this colour?

MAUREEN. Mm, it's nice.

JULIE. Sunshimmer gold. Do you think I should put some more on, for the stage lights, I mean?

MAUREEN. It's all right, what you've done. You don't want to look tarty.

JULIE. I wouldn't mind — the judges are all men aren't they? God, I'm bursting. I don't know how many bloody Babychams I've had now. And I ate soup for my tea as well.

MAUREEN. What, just soup?

JULIE. I never eat a lot before I go out — I feel bloated. I was too nervous anyway. I had tomato soup and a Raspberry Mivvi out of our freezer. Did I tell you we'd got a freezer? It's full of ice lollies and a packet of beefburgers. My Mum says it cost so much she can't afford any food for it. Funny word isn't it?

MAUREEN. What?

JULIE. Mivvi.

MAUREEN. My Mum wouldn't let me go out without a proper meal inside me.

JULIE. My Mum doesn't care. She lives on Consulate and Smokey Bacon crisps.

MAUREEN. My Mum says it's not fair to your stomach not to have a proper meal at teatime. It aggravates the lining because its expecting it.

JULIE. I could go out through the disco and go to the Ladies there. I don't want anybody to see me really. Shall I go?

MAUREEN. We always have three courses — soup or avocado on a weekend, then a main course, then a sweet or cheese and biscuits if it's my father's night for the Oddfellows.

JULIE. Hey — I won't be able to sing if this goes on. I'll just be jigging up and down with my legs crossed. Could be worse. I knew this girl, well you knew her, Caroline Pilling, you remember — she had red hair and matching legs — well, she was at this posh house once and she was bursting for a pee, and she didn't like to say where's the toilet, so she said could she wash her hands. And they showed her into this room with just a washbasin in — so she sat on it and it came away from the wall — can you imagine — I'd have been out the window me. (*She starts looking round for something to wee into.*)

MAUREEN. And if it's Saturday or we've got company, we'll have matchmakers or After Eights with our coffee. In the other room. It's no extra bother to have it in the other room, because we've a hatch.

JULIE. What can I do it into?

MAUREEN. What?

JULIE. Have a wee — I'm dying.

MAUREEN. You're not serious.

JULIE. I haven't the anatomy for a Babycham bottle, have I? (*Opens filing cabinet.*) Shall I do it here, file it under P? (*Opens cupboard.*) Hey there's a potty here — no it isn't. (*Finds an imitation straw boater.*) Still it's plastic. Keep guard for us Maureen — there might be a reporter coming.

MAUREEN. What are you going to do with it?

JULIE. Chuck it out the window or stick it back in the cupboard.

MAUREEN. Ooh, how horrible.

MAUREEN *stands disapprovingly at the door, her back to* JULIE.

JULIE. There's nobody coming is there?

MAUREEN. No.

Pause.

JULIE. Isn't it funny — you really want to and then you can't — no, we're all right. That's better. I'll climb up and open that window — you hand it up to me.

MAUREEN. I'm not going near it — I might catch something.

JULIE. I'll do it myself. (*Opens window.*) I daren't chuck it — There's loads of people on the pavement, and it's not even raining. I'll leave it on the window-sill and do it after. (*Climbs down.*) I feel great now. I'm having another Babycham — d'you want one?

MAUREEN. I'd better not.

JULIE. Why not? Go on.

MAUREEN. I'm terrible when I'm tiddly. One New Year's Eve I ended up doing the conga into the spare bedroom.

JULIE. Who with?

MAUREEN. My Mum and Dad. (*Takes a Babycham.*)

JULIE (*getting nervous again*). Are there any other singers in this, did that compère say?

MAUREEN. I don't know, I don't listen to other people's private conversations. It was you he was talking to.

JULIE. I know — I've got this thing, I can't listen when people are talking to me. I mean when they're telling me things like directions. They're going 'left at the library and behind the butcher's,' and I go yeah yeah right, and I haven't taken it in.

MAUREEN. Where's that?

JULIE. Eh?

MAUREEN. That's Hilda's Remnants, isn't it?

JULIE. What?

MAUREEN. Left at the library and behind the butcher's.

JULIE. I don't know — I was just saying. It was an i.e., I mean an e.g., I'm losing my voice. I should have had my hair done. I wanted a wash 'n' wear perm but I've spent up. They're a bit common them anyway.

MAUREEN. My father says that girls with perms look like barmy sheep. He said it in his speech at Oddfellow's Ladies' Night and quite a few people said hear hear. He's very dry my father. My mother had a fun fur, you know fun fur fabric, she won in a raffle on our caravan site. He said she looked like a polar bear. He said she was lucky it wasn't the hunting season or somebody might have shot her.

JULIE. Do you think it's all right, that dress?

MAUREEN. Looks a bit small.

JULIE. Well, it's tight-fitting. The woman in the shop said it should be like a second skin. I think she were a les. Lesbe friends?

MAUREEN. Looks too small to me.

JULIE. Bloody hell, it's a cabaret club, not an ante-natal clinic. That underskirt's too big for me — d'you want it?

MAUREEN (*taking it — it is obviously far too small for her*). Thanks. I don't think I can wear it though, actually.

JULIE. Why?

MAUREEN. My slips have to be anti-stat because of the electricity.

JULIE. My sister's like that. Get her in between a pair of nylon sheets and you could run a colour telly off her. (*Holds dress up.*) I'm not mad about this colour, but still, you don't dress to please yourself, do you? I don't know whether to wear a bra or not, what d'ye think?

MAUREEN. How can you not wear one?

JULIE. I hardly ever do, me.

MAUREEN. You used to at school.

JULIE. Well, everybody did then, didn't they. We all had our Dorothy Perkins half-cup wired. Oh no, you didn't, did you? You had those awful white cotton things with three fasteners. I hardly ever wear one now.

MAUREEN. You'll pay for it later.

JULIE (*starts to put dress on*). I'm not bothered — I'm going to shoot myself when I'm thirty-five. The thing is, if it's cold on stage my nipples might stand out.

MAUREEN. Julie!

JULIE. And one's bigger than the other, and it might be distracting. Is one of yours?

MAUREEN. I've never looked.

JULIE. I hadn't noticed about mine, but Dave said. He keeps threatening to measure them. He's a daft sod.

MAUREEN. When did he see them?

JULIE. Yesterday, most of last weekend when his Mum and Dad were away, whenever we do it; unless we're in his car in which case I keep my sweater on 'cos his heater's packed in.

MAUREEN. I didn't know you . . .

JULIE. What did you think we did? Community singing?

MAUREEN. Does your Mum know?

JULIE. I think finding Dave's underpants under one of the sofa cushions gave her a rough idea. Hey, what time is it?

MAUREEN *shows her watch.*

Will you test me on my words?

She gives MAUREEN *the music.*

'What good is sitting alone in your room, come hear the music play; life is a cabaret old chum, only a cabaret.'

MAUREEN. 'Come to.'

JULIE. What?

MAUREEN. 'Life is a cabaret old chum, come to the cabaret.' You said, *'only* a cabaret.'

JULIE. It doesn't matter. (*Mutters quickly to herself.*) Yes. Right. 'Put down the knitting

MAUREEN *keeps shaking her head.*

the book and the broom.' What's up — that's right. Now I know this bit.

MAUREEN. It's 'Come taste the wine, come hear the band.'

JULIE. (*snatches music off her and points*). It isn't — you go back to this bit, underneath the first bit. Then you go on to the bit you said.

MAUREEN. It seems a funny way to write it.

JULIE. You don't mind if I carry on?

MAUREEN. No.

JULIE. I've forgotten what I'm doing now.

MAUREEN. Well, according to you, it's 'Put down the knitting the book and the broom.'

JULIE. 'Put down the knitting the book and the broom, time for a holiday, life is a cabaret old chum, come to the cabaret.'

MAUREEN. 'Come taste the . . . '

JULIE. I know! I was just breathing in. 'Come taste the band, wine, come hear the band, come — something — celebrating, right this way your table's waiting.'

MAUREEN. 'Come blow the horn.'

JULIE. Yeah — I'll remember that. I only do the second verse of the next bit. 'Start by admitting from cradle to tomb isn't that long a stay — life is a cabaret old chum, only a cabaret old chum, so come to the cabaret.'

MAUREEN. You've missed some out.

JULIE. I haven't. What?

MAUREEN. Look. 'Isn't that long a (*Turns over.*) stay — life is a cabaret old chum, come to the cabaret, come taste the, ret, old chum.' Then 'only a cabaret etc. etc.'

JULIE. You don't do it like that. You go from here to there.

MAUREEN. Why?

JULIE. I don't know. There was a man playing the organ in the music shop, and he said that when you got to that blob, you missed out a bit, and went from the next blob.

MAUREEN. It seems a funny way of doing it.

JULIE (*sings*). 'Life is a cabaret old chum.'

MAUREEN. I thought there was something about Elsie in it.

JULIE. You what?

MAUREEN. I thought there was a bit in the song about a girl called Elsie. (*Thinks.*) I think she lived in Chelsea.

JULIE *pulls a 'Don't-know-and-don't-care' face.*

JULIE. It's funny, I've been up all night, and I don't feel tired. Haven't slept much since the audition — it's only about a week ago.

MAUREEN. Wednesday — ten days.

JULIE. I just read it in the paper and went straight there. I had
no music, I sang it without a piano, without a microphone,
nothing. They said afterwards with a voice like mine I didn't
need one. And then I got the letter the next morning saying
I'd passed the audition. (*Gets out much read letter.*) 'Most
impressed with your voice.' I've always had a good voice
though. I used to do Shirley Bassey when I was five with a
dessert spoon for a microphone. I shattered a liqueur glass
doing 'I, I who have nothing.' There was a bit of a row 'cos
it was one my Auntie Kathleen brought back from Ibiza
before her breakdown.

MAUREEN. What was that?

JULIE. I don't really know. They only talk about it on Boxing
Day. Give us a fag. You know if you win and get a job in all
the Bunter's Clubs, like I told you — you know how much you
get paid?

MAUREEN. No.

JULIE. £50 a night. If you only took Sundays off that's £300
a week.

MAUREEN. Somebody's been having you on — singers don't
earn that much.

JULIE. I'd get a flat in Manchester. No, I'd live in the Piccadilly
Plaza, then I wouldn't have to wash up. I'd have a mini with
black windows.

MAUREEN. You can't drive.

JULIE. I'd have a black chauffeur to match.

MAUREEN. You don't even know you'll win this, let alone the
Final.

JULIE. Even if I don't I might get spotted.

MAUREEN. Who by?

JULIE. You know that compère? He told me a BBC producer
quite often comes in on Friday nights. And — the man on the
door who I was talking to last week comes from Birmingham

and knows the floor manager off New Faces. So you see . . .

MAUREEN. Even if somebody saw you, they don't take girls from offices to be on television.

JULIE. They do — what about Pam Ayres?

MAUREEN. She probably knew someone.

JULIE. Slept her way to the top? Come in Miss Ayres, get your corsets off and read us a poem about hedgehogs?

MAUREEN. I didn't mean sleeping . . .

JULIE. I'd do that though. I would.

MAUREEN. Go all the way with a man, just for a job?

JULIE. Course I would. As long as he didn't have bad breath. That's one thing about not being married yet — I don't have to do it in the morning. That was the worst thing about when we went camping — it was like some bleeding Eastern Ritual, weaving about trying to avoid each other's faces.

MAUREEN. I thought you had to take your Mark with you.

JULIE. We did, we kept sending him out for milk. Every time we fancied a bit, we'd say 'go and get us some milk, Mark.' We had so much in the end we had to bury it. Can you fasten my shoes, I daren't bend over. You've never done it, have you, Maur?

MAUREEN. I wouldn't know what to do.

JULIE. You don't do anything — men do all the work.

MAUREEN (standing up). I don't know what you're worried about this contest for, you're getting married when Dave gets his promotion, aren't you?

JULIE. Yes.

MAUREEN. It's a pity he couldn't come with you tonight.

JULIE. I didn't want him to. I wanted to have a good time.

MAUREEN. Just going to the loo. He's really nice. (Leaving) Dave, I think.

JULIE. He's a nice lad. (She sings:)

Fourteen Again

I want to be fourteen again
Sex was just called number ten
I was up to seven and a half.
Boys were for love, girls were for fun
You burst out laughing if you saw a nun,
Sophistication was a sports car and a chiffon scarf.

I want to be fourteen again,
Tattoo myself with a fountain pen,
Pretend to like the taste of rum and coke,
Chuck my school hat in a bush,
Spit on my mascara brush,
Buy Consulate and teach myself to smoke.

I want to be fourteen again,
Free rides on the waltzer off the fairground men
For a promise of a snog the last night of the fair,
French kissing as the kiosks shut
Behind the generators with your coconut,
The coloured lights reflected in the Brylcreem on his hair.

I want to be fourteen again
For all the things I didn't know then,
When I was funny I was famous, I was never ignored,
I was crazy Jules, I had a laugh,
I had Ilia Kuriakin's autograph,
I had no idea you could wake up feeling bored.

At the end of the song, JULIE *takes out a cassette player and switches it on. 'Twenty Disco Hits' or similar. She starts to dance, admiring herself in the mirror and touching up her make-up.* MAUREEN *comes in, rubbing her elbow.*

MAUREEN. A man with a suitcase banged right into me.

JULIE. That'll be the photographer. There's a reporter coming round, you know, to interview me before the show. Do I look all right? I hate having my photograph taken. Better start getting used to it. You know, if I win, when Derek comes round with the wages, I'll say forget it, I'm worth £300 a week now. And Mr Brennand can get stuffed, and Mingy Martha,

and Mrs Kawolski — and my Mum. I'll say I don't care if
your bloody legs drop off tomorrow, I'm leaving. And Dave . . .

MAUREEN. Not Dave.

JULIE. Well, he can run after me for a change.

There is a knock on the door. JULIE *switches off the cassette.*

GEORGE (*off*). Ladies all decent?

JULIE. That'll be the reporter — give us a fag. Come in.

GEORGE FINDLEY *comes in wearing a dinner-jacket, with
his friend ARTHUR, who is pushing a decorated tea trolley
covered in magician's props.*

GEORGE. I'll just put this here — it won't be in your way, will
it?

JULIE. No.

GEORGE. You're not doing any limbering up, or anything of
that nature?

JULIE. Not unless Maureen decides to have another crack at
the Military Two Step.

GEORGE. Dancing Team, are you?

MAUREEN. No, Julie's singing tonight.

GEORGE. Singer, is it? I thought when your friend said the
Military Two Step, I thought you must be part of a troupe,
like. Where do you sing, love?

JULIE. I haven't done a lot, really. I've just started, really. I
work in an office at the moment — just till it picks up a bit.

GEORGE. I thought I didn't recognise you — not been on the
telly?

JULIE. Not yet — I'm hoping to get on New Faces soon.

GEORGE. Now I've not seen that one. Have you seen that one,
Arthur?

ARTHUR. We don't get that one on our telly.

GEORGE. How's that, Arthur?

ARTHUR. It's got no plug.

GEORGE. I shall do that one tonight if you're not careful.
   And does your friend sing?

MAUREEN. No, I don't. My father says . . .

GEORGE. Arthur here's the one for singing. Ey, ask him where
   he sings. Go on — ask him where he sings.

   JULIE *laughs*.

MAUREEN. Where d'you sing?

ARTHUR. Bath, back seat of charas, and toilets with no lock
   on' door.

GEORGE. I always like that one.

JULIE. Do you know what time it starts?

GEORGE. I don't. I've no doubt someone will come for me
   when they want me. Are you — er — watching it from
   here, are you?

JULIE. No, I'm singing tonight.

GEORGE. Are you, be gum. I didn't know there were singists
   on tonight. I thought it was just those punk rockers on.
   You're not with them, are you?

JULIE. No, they're on afterwards.

GEORGE. I thought you weren't with them, shall I tell you how
   I know? You've no safety pin through your nose. Well, if we're
   fellow artistes, I should introduce myself. George Findley,
   and this is my helper for the night, Arthur Hall.

   GEORGE *sings 'Pals' with* ARTHUR:

   Pals

   Pals —
   No one can hurt you or mess you about
   If you've got a pal, I've found.
   Pals —
   They won't desert you, of that there's no doubt,
   Who needs a gal around?

And if you're lonely and the skies are grey,
It looks like just another rainy day,
Your best pal can drive the blues away.
He'll tell you the sun is shining,
He'll point out the silver lining.

Pals —
We stick together like some patent glue,
We can't be pulled apart.
Pals —
Birds of a feather, the feeling just grew,
Friendship comes from the heart.

And if you find yourself across the sea,
Fighting a war for home and liberty,
You're feeling homesick as can be —
One voice says, 'Cheer up, will ya?'
One pal can make it all familiar.

They dance to music of one verse and chorus.

Pals —
One thing about them they always go shares,
A million pounds or a bun.
Pals —
We're nowhere without them, a pal really cares,
And we wouldn't have so much fun.

JULIE. I'm Julie Stephens, and this is Maureen.

GEORGE. Stephens — I used to know a Stephens — lived two
doors down from my mother's. He was a terrible nuisance,
because he'd this very large pig he kept in the back yard,
and he was for ever knocking on the back door while you
were having tea or dinner, and saying 'can you spare me a bit
of dinner for my pig?' You didn't know him, did you?

JULIE. No — we live in a bungalow.

GEORGE. This is before the war I'm talking about now. My
mother used to say the amount she'd given that pig, it owed
her at least two rashers of bacon and a pound of sausages.

ARTHUR. And did you get them, George?

GEORGE. We never did. Because — the very day that pig was killed, my mother was run over by a dustcart in front of the reference library, and was in the Infirmary for three months. On liquids.

ARTHUR. So she couldn't have eaten them, even if she'd had them George, had you thought of that.

GEORGE. She was never the same when she came home. She couldn't zip her dresses up at the back — that kind of thing. She was very low. Well Arthur, shall I check my props, or shall I go on and surprise myself?

ARTHUR. I should check your props, George.

JULIE. What are you going to do?

GEORGE. Magic. Comedy magic. I think it goes down better if you make it light-hearted. Oh, and banjo finale.

JULIE. Who do you think'll win?

GEORGE. Beg your pardon?

JULIE. Who do you think'll win this . . . contest . . . heat?

GEORGE. Is it a contest? I didn't know that? Did you know that Arthur?

ARTHUR. I didn't, George — no, nobody told me that. Or if they did, I didn't hear them.

JULIE. What did you think you were doing then?

GEORGE. I do a lot of these little shows round and about. I got this one winning the Pensioners' Talent Afternoon at the Floral Hall last week.

ARTHUR. He had 101 marks out a possible 130 — and the Senior Citizens' Saxophonistes only managed an 89.

GEORGE. Just lucky, that's all, Arthur. I think Nell's new dress helped.

ARTHUR. Well, we shall have to manage without it tonight.

GEORGE. I bet you've been wondering where my wife is, eh?

GIRLS *smile politely.*

GEORGE. She would normally be here, but I'm making do with Arthur tonight.

ARTHUR. Not often you see a magician with a male assistant. I should have brought Nell's dress.

GEORGE. Now now, Arthur, you'll have the young ladies thinking you're one of those . . .

ARTHUR. Oh aye — don't think I'm a nancy boy.

GEORGE. Nell would be here normally, no doubt of it. But we've had a little bit of a mix-up with our bookings, and she's had to be at the Drill Hall. It's the Hard-of-Hearing Beetle Drive. Nell's entertaining during the refreshment break. She's got a bit of a cold tonight, so I've told her 'Sally,' 'Jerusalem,' 'Bless This House,' and straight home to bed.

JULIE. Who do you think'll win?

GEORGE. Jacky James. No doubt of it. If he's in it at all, like. I've seen him outside. He's marvellous — easily as good as Norman Vaughan. We're about set up, Arthur. Shall we go back and sit with the others for a bit — not much doing here.

ARTHUR. George's fans are here tonight. You'll hear 'em screaming when he comes on.

GEORGE. He's only kidding. It's just a few people from the Sixty Years Young Club. They like to give support. Are you right, Arthur?

ARTHUR. I am, George.

They leave.

I might have a dance. What is it they do now — the bump is it?

MAUREEN. He's really good, Jacky James. We saw him in the panto last year. He did a ventriloquist sort of thing with a little puppy. It was very amusing.

Pause.

How's your Cliff? Is he still seeing the Probation Officer?

JULIE. Army.

MAUREEN. I hope he's not like those terrible boys you see on the Inter-City, shouting and being vulgar. Where's he stationed?

JULIE. He's on special attachment to British Rail — he goes up and down train corridors with a green canvas suitcase, insulting people. I'm going getting a drink. (*Stands up, trips up.*) I can't get used to these shoes.

MAUREEN. You should always wear shoes in before a special occasion. My mother's cousin — I call her Auntie, but she's actually a cousin — got one of her stilettoes stuck in the grating outside the UCP. She wasn't used to them, having been a nun (*Trying to make the story more interesting.*) and she was in a bit of a hurry trying to get in the queue for Paulden's sale — they were having startling reductions on formica kitchen units.

JULIE. How come she stopped being a nun?

MAUREEN. They were always having tomato soup, and she lost her faith.

JULIE *leaves.* MAUREEN *wanders round, poking about in* JULIE's *make-up, sucks in her stomach, looks in the mirror. The door opens, and she sits down quickly.* MEL *comes in.*

MEL. Hello — you must be (*Looks at piece of paper.*) Judy?

MAUREEN. No, I'm not singing. My friend's just gone to the bar.

MEL. Do you happen to have her music at all, love? What's the matter?

MAUREEN. Just thought I recognised you from somewhere. (*Hands him the music.*)

MEL. Dear oh dear oh dear, when will they learn?

MAUREEN. Sorry?

MEL. Take no notice of me, love. I've had to play this so many times. When will girls learn to choose something a bit more original? I'm the organist. Still, what's the odds. Nobody listens.

MAUREEN. I'm sure they'll listen to my friend. She's got a very loud voice.

MEL. No, they're all as thick as two short planks out there tonight. Jacky might get them, but I can't see anyone else managing it.

   JULIE — *with drinks on a tray* — *pushes the door open with her back.*

JULIE. I got a rum and coke and a port — which do you want? (*Sees* MEL).

MEL. Julie!

JULIE. What are you doing here?

MEL. I'm playing organ in the trio. So you're singing here tonight?

JULIE. Yes.

MEL. How are you? You're looking fabulous. You've had your hair cut. How long is it since I've seen you?

JULIE. Eight years.

MEL. Must be — yeah, must be about eight. I thought about you. I wondered if you'd be coming into the Club at all. I always listen out on Ladies' Night for that voice! It's great to see you.

JULIE. How long have you been back?

MEL. A few months, on and off, since my father died. We're buying a house here, if the deal goes through. Long business, trying to buy a house.

   Pause.

MAUREEN. You two know each other then?

MEL. This is my first steady girlfriend you're looking at here. And you still look smashing. You've lost weight, it suits you. You were a bit on the chubby side before, more like your friend here. Now — business. Your music.

JULIE. It's this.

MEL. Nice. Fabulous song. I bet you sing it really well.

JULIE. Someone told me that this music's lower than it is on the record, so can you play it higher? They've written it here — 'key of F#' — is that all right? .

MEL. Not really. You see it's been written in E♭, so it's a bit of an awkward transposition. I think I've got it in C, it's a bit lower. But I'm sure you'll be fine. Got your drum and bass parts?

JULIE. No, I've only got this.

MEL. Just you and me and my organ, then, Jules, eh? Like old times, ha ha. (*Preparing to leave.*) Anyway — back to the bar. Have a bit of a chinwag later, perhaps, Julie? Lovely.

MEL *leaves.*

MAUREEN. I'm sure I remember him, what's his name?

JULIE. Mel.

MAUREEN. Was that Mel? That used to pick you up from school in a sports car?

JULIE. Yeah. A red one.

MAUREEN. That's right. Fancy that.

JULIE. I'd better go and phone Dave — he's probably smoking himself to death worrying how I've got on.

MAUREEN. I didn't think he was that bothered, by the sound of things.

JULIE. Oh he is. Sent me roses and a good luck card this morning.

MAUREEN. Let's have a look.

JULIE. I couldn't bring it — it's about three foot square. The postman had to ring the doorbell, it wouldn't go through the letterbox.

JULIE *goes out to the phone, dials a number. She puts in 10p and speaks in a slightly posher voice.*

Hello, could I speak to David, please? It's Julie. Oh, I thought as it was Friday, you wouldn't have gone to bed . . . sorry . . .

not really, I just wanted a word with David, is he in? . . . I'm
in a cabaret club . . . Yes you can phone back, I'll give you the
number, 8397224 . . . I will hear it, I'll stay by the phone . . .
right, thank you very much, sorry to have got you out of
bed . . . yes, thank you Mrs Walters. Bye.

*Goes back into the room, lights a cigarette, picks up her
drink.*

MAUREEN. That was quick.

JULIE. That was his mother — I forgot they'd got a phone in the
bleeding bedroom. 'David's in the garage with some friends,
is it important?'

MAUREEN. What are they doing in the garage at this time of
night?

JULIE. It's not really a garage — well, half of it is — the other
half's got a billiard table in and a darts board. He has his mates
in there so nobody does anything nasty like walking on her
carpets, or breathing any of her oxygen.

MAUREEN. Is she very fussy?

JULIE. Fussy? You have to leave your shoes in the cloakroom
on a piece of newspaper, then she provides you with a pair of
slippers. She doesn't like me, so I always get the folded over
tartan ones with the fuzzy bobbles. If you want to smoke, you
have to go out onto the patio. God knows what she'd do if
anybody farted.

MAUREEN. Julie!

JULIE. She'd probably jump up and start attacking your bum
with air freshener.

MAUREEN. Is she horrible to you?

JULIE. She looks at me like I'm something spat out by their
mynah bird. But she's very nice. 'More tea, Julie? Corn on
the cob, Julie? Mouth or bum, Julie?'

The phone rings.

MAUREEN. He took his time.

JULIE. It'll have taken his Mum ages dragging her coffin down

the stairs. (*She goes out and answers the phone.*) Hello? Yes —
hyah Dave . . . Nothing, thought I'd ring, what you doing? . . .
Who's there? . . . Who invited her? . . . Oh, did you? . . . I
don't *want* anything — thought you might be interested to
know how I was getting on . . . I'm at Bunter's . . . For the
talent contest — I told you . . . Yeah, singing, well done, well
remembered . . . I've not been on yet. I've been hanging round
ages — it's really funny. I'm in this pokey old room. Backstage
is nothing like the rest of it, you know how posh it is . . .
What's happening? What you laughing at? . . . Who else is
there? . . . Well, look, shall I ring you later, when they're all
gone — we haven't had a proper talk for ages. You'll want to
know how I've got on, won't you? . . . It should be over by
eleven . . . You phone me then, here, if it's going to wake her
up . . . Well, Michael's got a phone, hasn't he? . . . Well, I'll
ring you then, first thing tomorrow morning, tell you how I
got on . . . How long are you sleeping in? . . . Who's that
laughing? . . . What? . . . I can't hear you. Hello? Dave?

JULIE *puts the phone down, and dials the same number, then
immediately puts the phone down again.* MEL *comes in,
carrying a band-book with J.J. on it.*

MEL. Jules — you haven't seen Jacky James anywhere around,
have you? There's something I want to run through with
him. (*She shakes her head.*) God, it takes me back, seeing
you. We had a lot of fun, didn't we?

MAUREEN *sings the first verse of* 'He Wouldn't Remember Me'.

Julie had a lover
He signed his letters 'lover',
She passed them round her friends at break.
She didn't show them Maureen,
So Maureen said 'how boring'
And ate cake.
Triumph was written on Julie's face
Mel's name was on her pencil case
She'd discuss his finer points for hours.
Maureen, sexy as a doormat,
Found solace with *Fourth Form at*

Mallory Towers.
He was Melvyn during office hours
But he was Mel at night;
When he would often quite surprise himself
Saying 'I love you, I really do, and I won't let you down'.

JULIE. Haven' you got anything to say?

MEL. Sorry?

JULIE. About pissing off and leaving me pregnant?

MEL. Sorry about that.

Pause.

It was obviously a bit awkward for me: didn't want my
boss finding out I'd knocked up a schoolgirl. And I had a long
talk with my family — they were fantastic, really helpful, and
we all thought . . . it would be . . . better to go.

MAUREEN *sings the second verse of* 'He Wouldn't Remember
Me'.

Mel was very randy
So his car came in quite handy,
Well stocked up with Durex and a comb.
She had love bites round her nipple,
Maureen had Raspberry Ripple
At home.
Half the girls were jealous
The other half said 'Tell us
Does it hurt and what's it really like?'
She brags 'Eight times on Sunday,
Then went out on Monday
On my bike.
He was Melvyn during office hours
But he was Mel at night;
When he would often quite surprise himself,
Saying 'I love you, I really do, and I won't let you down,

MEL. No point getting heavy about it this late in the day. I mean
an abortion's not much to get steamed up about these days.
Cath's sister had one; and she helped us paint our kitchen
ceiling the week after.

JULIE. I didn't have one. I didn't know anything about it then.
By the time I'd seen the doctor it was too late. I was just
running about in a panic — trying to remember when my last
period was, buying penny royal from horrible little backstreet
shops. My mother hit me when she found out.

MAUREEN *sings the third verse of* 'He Wouldn't Remember Me'.

She was happy going steady,
He gave her perfume, talc, a teddy,
Gifts arrived by nearly every post.
Most mornings you could hear the noise
Of Jules unwrapping cute soft toys
And crunching toast.
He could do Spike Milligan's 'Hello folks',
Had a pleasing line in dirty jokes,
Nice-looking and nearly twenty-three.
Julie's got a lucky star
A boyfriend with his own sports car
Whoopee.
He was Melvyn during office hours
But he was Mel at night;
When he would often quite surprise himself
Saying 'I love you, I really do, and I won't let you down'.

MEL. What did you have?

JULIE. A boy. Justin.

MEL. That's a smashing name. Did he look like me at all?

JULIE. Never saw him. They tried to bring him in, but I said no.

MEL. And what have you been doing all this time?

JULIE. Well, I left school. I'd failed most of my 'O' levels, what
with one thing and another. Or the other. I couldn't face doing
them again — nobody knew about it or anything, but, well,
you go off things, don't you? I've done a lot of things:
receptionist, switchboard, filing clerk, forecourt attendant.
I've been at Benson's for nearly three years now. I work with
Maureen — The girl in there.

MEL. My mother tells me you're engaged. Dave Walters — he's
doing very well for himself, I hear.

JULIE. Yeah, OK. We'll probably get a house soon.

MEL. You can't beat having your own place.

> ARTHUR *dashes past them, into the room and out again, clutching the props for Candle Thru Arm.*

ARTHUR. You should come out and watch George do this — it's marvellous. Can you imagine, a lighted candle going right through someone's arm? We're having a grand time. (*Dashes off.*)

MEL. You get nutters like that in every Talent Contest. Opera singers in wheelchairs — they're living in a dream world. You done them before?

JULIE. When I was eight I won five bob off Leslie Crowther at Southport for singing 'Catch a Falling Star'. I'd love to do it full time.

MEL. I wouldn't. It would drive me up the bloody wall.

JULIE. I thought this was your proper job.

MEL. It's just a way of earning a bit of cash that the taxman can't get his grubby hands on. And of course it means I see more of Cath than I otherwise would. I have to keep an eye on her. Men find her pretty irresistible.

JULIE. How do you mean?

MEL. My wife's Cathy Christmas — she has the residency here. She's doing pretty well for herself, too; gets quite a lot of radio work, Radio 2 mostly, and she's in a new TV talent show on BBC Scotland next month.

JULIE. Is she singing before me?

MEL. No way. I mean, I'm not being rude, love, but if she went on first you'd really notice the difference — incredible voice. You'll be on just after the disco, when people are getting the drinks in before the cabaret.

JULIE. Right.

MEL. You're not worried, are you? It's a laugh, anyway, isn't it? Something to tell your pals tomorrow.

JULIE. Specially if I win.

MEL. Well, these things — it's not really a case of how well you do. There's no clapometer or anything.

JULIE. What do you mean?

MEL. Nothing, but Maurice who runs this club is also a manager, and he manages Jacky James. It may not work like that tonight, of course. Anyway, I must go and find Cath.

JULIE. Are you playing for her as well?

MEL. I'm nowhere near good enough for her. (*Starts to leave.*) She has her own pianist. If you meet my wife, we're just old friends, eh? Ciao.

GEORGE *and* ARTHUR *come in,* GEORGE *with a pint of mild, and* ARTHUR *with a Guinness.* MEL *stops to speak to them.* GEORGE *and* ARTHUR *are having a good time.*

ARTHUR. The woman is mad. There's no other explanation. I've never played Bingo in Morecambe in my life.

GEORGE. They can't keep their hands off you, you see, Arthur, it's your sex appeal.

ARTHUR. She's probably mixing me up with that Sacha Distel.

GEORGE. Oh, aye. She probably saw him in Morecambe, playing Bingo.

ARTHUR. You may be right about my sex appeal. I was once taken for Ronald Colman in the middle of Blackpool Illuminations.

GEORGE. Before they switched them on, you mean?

JULIE (*to* GEORGE). Excuse me, did you happen to notice a Ladies' toilet on your way here?

GEORGE. Yes, love, back towards the ballroom . . .

ARTHUR. Disco, George. (*Sings:*) We're Discos, we're Discos, we're KP Discos!

GEORGE. And it's in a little alcove on the left.

JULIE. Thank you. (*She leaves.*)

MEL. Excuse me, (*Looks at piece of paper.*) Mr Finney, Comedy Magician?

GEORGE. Findley. With banjo finale.

MEL. I'm the organist.

GEORGE. How do.

MEL. I don't know if you're needing any music at all.

GEORGE. That would be very nice.

MEL (*preparing to leave*). Just leave that to us, and we'll play you on and off.

GEORGE (*rummaging in pocket*). In fact, I've got it on me. (*He produces a tatty piece of music all taped together with stamp paper, covered in instructions.*) I'll just take you through it, though it's fairly straightforward. Drumroll to start. Eight bars 'Anything Goes' — you know, 'in olden days a glimpse of stocking etc.' Then I tell a couple of jokes using my bucket. Then on the second one — on the line 'no thanks, I'm only waiting' — you play these two bars here to finish off. They're on page two, but they actually come after this bit. Then four bars of 'A Pretty Girl is like a Melody', as I introduce Arthur. Normally that would be Nell, my wife, so if you could do a couple of discords here, as he comes on — to point the joke, like. I'll write that in for you. (*Licks a stumpy pencil, and scribbles on the music with it.*) Then it's 'Run, Rabbit, Run', while I'm doing a couple of rabbit-type anecdotes, and of course the top-hat comedy rabbit production routine. Then vamp the intro to 'Old Black Magic', while I sort myself out. Then I do a couple of volunteer card tricks. Then cut this, Handel's 'Water Music'; I'm not doing that, 'cos Nell's taken the Thermos to the Beetle Drive. So it's straight on to 'You Need Hands', for the Wrist Chopper. I'm not doing that, or that, so you cut right down to the bottom of the page for 'She Was One Of The Early Birds' — that's the old latex budgie routine. Then if you see me getting out my banjo, that means I'm doing an encore — either be 'If Women Like Them Like Men Like Those, Why Don't Women Like Me', or 'Ole Man River'. All right, son? (*Turning to leave.*) Or 'Swanee'. Which isn't down here, but just busk along in F. I think it goes (*Singing in rhythm with the tune.*) 'F, F, F Augmented, F Augmented, B♭ Old Swanee.' Don't worry, anyway.

MEL *leaves.* GEORGE *and* ARTHUR *go into the room.*
MAUREEN *is eating chocolate, which she quickly puts away*
when they come in.

ARTHUR. Do you think he got all that, George?

GEORGE. I doubt it, Arthur. These young chaps sound as if
they're playing with their backsides.

ARTHUR. Did you get through to Nell — I forgot to ask you.

GEORGE. Aye. She was just off to bed. I said, I hope you've
got a hot drink. She said, 'Yes, I have, the last of your whisky.'
I said, I hope I'm not coming home to a drunken woman. She
said if I didn't want to come home, I could aways lodge the
night with Doris Hargreaves.

ARTHUR. By, I wouldn't — I'd rather pay tuppence to swing
over a rope. She's soft in the head — I've never played Bingo in
Morecambe. In fact, I'm damn sure I've never played Bingo.

GEORGE. Now, you've played that with Nell and I. They weren't
calling it Bingo at the time — Housey Housey. I won a pair of
baby's bootees and a tin of toffees, if I remember rightly.

ARTHUR. Oh yes. Box of chocolates, you won, not toffees.

GEORGE. Was it?

ARTHUR. Weekend, a box of Weekend.

GEORGE. That's a funny thing to remember. How come you
remember that?

ARTHUR. Because they were all bloody jellies, and I couldn't
manage them. How was Nell, anyway? Is she coming to Sunset
House tomorrow?

GEORGE. I don't think she's up to it. It's a fair way to go, and
we've a lot of jobs on next week.

ARTHUR. You'll be after my services again, will you?

GEORGE. Afraid so. Now, it won't be too difficult. They're all old
folk, so I shan't be doing any of the quick-fire stuff, no bucket
jokes, nothing like that. Do you think you could manage the
mind-reading?

ARTHUR. I don't know. It was a bit dicey last time. If it hadn't been a Home for the Aged Deaf, I don't think we'd have got away with it.

GEORGE. Let's have a little go, and see how much you can remember. If it's no good, I'll do the Omelette Pan, Candle Thru Arm, and Memories of Jack Warner. Want to give us a hand, love?

MAUREEN. What do I have to do?

GEORGE. You sit here and be the audience — I'll blindfold myself (*Does so, now speaking in a different way.*) I place the blindfold over my eyes and request my assistant to tie it tightly at the back. Thank you, Arthur. I can now see nothing at all, Ladies and Gentlemen. I will now ask my assistant, Arthur, to pass amongst you.

ARTHUR *does comedy 'Passing amongst you' impressions.* MAUREEN *is getting a bit giggly.*

Arthur — I sense you are now standing by a beautiful young lady — am I correct?

ARTHUR. You are correct. (*To* MAUREEN:) It's psychological, that. You stand next to some ugly old battleaxe, and she's flattered.

GEORGE. I would now like that young lady to hand my assistant Arthur any article of her choice.

MAUREEN *opens her bag, and brings out a small make-up mirror.*

Are you holding the article, Arthur?

ARTHUR. I am. Now, please tell me, if you can, what it is I am holding.

GEORGE. A pair of glasses.

ARTHUR. Sorry, George. If you can, please tell me now what it is I am holding.

GEORGE. A mirror!

ARTHUR. Quite correct. (*Mimes to* MAUREEN *to give him*

something else — she hands him a hanky.) Please inform me, if possible, now, what it is I have been handed.

GEORGE. A hanky!

ARTHUR. And, what is the colour, pray?

GEORGE. The colour is white!

ARTHUR. Quite correct!

GEORGE (*taking blindfold off*). Not bad, eh?

MAUREEN. It's very good. How do you do it?

GEORGE. I can't tell you that, love. I'm not allowed. Magic Circle.

MAUREEN. Oh, right.

GEORGE. It's good, though, isn't it?

MAUREEN. Yes, it is.

GEORGE. And you don't know how it's done, do you?

MAUREEN. No. Very clever.

GEORGE. Yes, it is clever. It's only a trick, like, when you know it — I don't actually read minds — but it's baffling isn't it?

MAUREEN. Yes, very.

GEORGE. I thought we'd baffled you. Do you want to see another one?

MAUREEN. Yes.

JULIE *comes in.*

Where've you been?

JULIE. What you doing?

GEORGE. Come here, young lady.

JULIE. Why? (*Going over to him.*) What you doing?

GEORGE. Here — put your hand through this.

JULIE. What you going to do?

GEORGE. I'm going to put a lighted candle through your arm.

JULIE. You are not.

GEORGE. It won't hurt.

JULIE. Thank you very much. (*Pulling faces at* MAUREEN.)

GEORGE *puts a candle through the tube on* JULIE's *arm.*

Ow, you're burning me.

GEORGE (*squatting down, and peering through the hole in the tube*). It's still a bit bent, you know, Arthur, I shall have to take it round to the works.

JULIE. (*rubbing her arm*). You all right, Maureen? He hasn't tried to saw you in half, or anything?

MAUREEN. I've had my mind read.

JULIE. I bet that didn't take long — good joke, well done me. Cilla Black can't last for ever.

ARTHUR. I don't suppose there's time for me to run through my card trick, is there?

GEORGE. I'm sure there's time. That compère fella's not turned up yet. I'm sure the young ladies would like to see it. Eh?

JULIE } (*nudge each other*). Yeah.
MAUREEN

ARTHUR. You don't want to see my card trick. Six Card Repeat, it's called. You don't want to see that.

GEORGE. They do, Arthur, look at them. Better than pop groups, this, isn't it?

JULIE } Mmmmmm.
MAUREEN

ARTHUR. All right then, if everybody wants to see it, I don't mind. Now, I'm no David Nixon, and I've only been at this a couple of months — not like George here. Don't be expecting anything like, what's that young chap that says 'you're going to like this, you're not going to like it very much, but you're going to like it?'

JULIE } Paul Daniels.
MAUREEN

ARTHUR. Well, I'm not as good as him.

GEORGE. Taller though.

ARTHUR. I'm certainly taller.

GEORGE. Come on, Arthur — now, remember what I've told you — this is a good chance, this, for you.

The two go into a huddle, as GEORGE *helps* ARTHUR *arrange his cards.*

GEORGE. Are you ready?

ARTHUR (*nods*). Ladies and Gentlemen — I hope you don't mind me calling you that, it's only in fun. Ooh.

Turns to GEORGE *and whispers a question.* GEORGE *nods and encourages him on.*

I hope you don't mind me calling you that, it's only in fun. Yesterday, I bumped into an old fakir. He was hopping mad, because somebody had taken the nails out of his bed, and he couldn't get a wink of sleep. Actually, in the end, he spent most of the night under the bed. I said 'What do you feel like?' He said 'a little potty.' In fact, he was so potty, he insisted on showing me a card trick. (*Takes cards out of pocket.*) It was with six cards. (*Removes rubber bands from cards and throws them away.* GEORGE *picks them up and puts them away in a tin.*) One, two, three, four, five, and one is six. Then, very slowly, this fakir, — he was called a fakir, because he had a fake ear — he discarded one, two, three, (*Does so.*), and, believe it or not, he still had one, two, three, four, five, and one is six! I said 'That's amazing!' (GEORGE *is mouthing the words along with* ARTHUR, *as* JULIE *and* MAUREEN *become more and more bored.*) and he said 'There's nothing to it' — he had a Lancashire accent just like mine — in fact he also looked very like me — he said 'There's nothing to it'. You take one, two, three, four, five, and one is six cards — you very slowly discard one, two and three, (*Does so.*) and believe it or believe it not, you still have one, two, three, four, five, and one is six. I said 'I think I'm getting the hang of it now,' so I put down the garden gate I was holding — I'd taken it out of the woman next-door's garden

— well she's always taking offence! — said 'I think I can do this trick now,' I take one, two, three, four, five, and one is six cards — I discard one two three, and I have one, two, three. Then there's a comedy ending, isn't there, George?

GEORGE. Aye. It should be here next week. I've ordered it.

The COMPÈRE *comes in.*

COMPÈRE. Mr. Findley? I'd like you to go on first, if you would.

GEORGE. I've no objection. Arthur, have you any objection?

COMPÈRE (*ignoring them*). There's no rush, but I'd like you to take your things to the other side of the stage. Our Stage Manager Mike will be over there, and you can tell him what you need in the way of tables, chairs, lighting . . . You can go through this door here.

Indicating stage door. GEORGE *and* ARTHUR *wheel their trolley through.*

It's Julie, the little girl with the big voice. Feeling all right, Julie?

JULIE. I'm a bit nervous.

COMPÈRE. Don't worry — you'll be fine. Shall I give you an old showbiz tip? Deep breaths. Marvellous. Cigarette? Well, how do you like Bunter's?

JULIE. It's nice.

COMPÈRE. And how do you like backstage?

JULIE. It's all right.

COMPÈRE. It may look grotty to you, but it's what backstage is about, and I wouldn't have it any other way. I'm just a sentimental old pro, take no notice of me. Still like to work here, Julie?

JULIE. Oh yes.

COMPÈRE. What we'd like you to do now. — you've met Mel, our organist? He's got your music? There's a piano in the Henry VIII Grill Room over there — it's closed at the moment, some silly old bag insisted on inspecting the kitchens. We'd like you

just to run though the song a couple of times — I think that
gives you a bit more confidence and a better chance. OK?

JULIE. Right. Thank you.

COMPÈRE. Hang on — you are a little eager beaver, aren't you?
Now I've got to take down your particulars, as the actress said
to the bishop. We want to give you a nice intro, don't we?
Now, it's Julie . . .

JULIE. Stephens. P.H. (*He writes on a card.*)

COMPÈRE. And you're what, twenty-one, twenty-two?

MAUREEN (*with* JULIE). It's like a bit off that Palmolive advert.

JULIE (*with* MAUREEN). You sound like the Palmolive advert.
I'm twenty-four.

COMPÈRE. I'll just say 'young girl'. Twenty-four's a bit . . . Well,
you're no Lena Zavaroni, are you? Now there's a great voice.
Now, you are an amateur, aren't you, love? Non-Equity,
non-M.U.?

JULIE (*not understanding*). Well . . .

COMPÈRE. You don't sing for a living?

JULIE. No, I'm a secretary.

COMPÈRE. Mm, no laughs there. Got any hobbies? Funny
boyfriends?

JULIE. I don't think I've got any hobbies, have I?

MAUREEN. Shoplifting.

JULIE (*to* MAUREEN). I do not! (*to* COMPÈRE:) I don't.
(COMPÈRE *is not amused, waiting.*) I like reading, cooking,
and camping.

MAUREEN *laughs.*

COMPÈRE. Fresh air fiend, eh? OK — and what are you singing?

JULIE. Cabaret.

COMPÈRE. That's from 'Cabaret', is it? Liza Minelli — there's a
good voice. Not surprising, with Judy Garland for a mother.
You haven't got a famous mother, have you?

JULIE. No, but my Auntie Kathleen married someone out of Brian Poole and the Tremeloes.

COMPÈRE. Nice boys, played here many a time.

JULIE. I suppose you've met lots of famous people?

COMPÈRE. Darling — I don't care if a person's famous or not. If they interest me, I'll talk to them. If they don't — I don't care who they are, I don't want to know.

MAUREEN. Do you know Morecambe and Wise?

COMPÈRE. Oh yeah. I tell you something — I don't think they're all that funny.

JULIE. I'll go and find the — Grill Room, was it?

COMPÈRE. Don't panic, I will take you there, my love. (*To* MAUREEN:) Perhaps you could stay here, er, could you, keep an eye on the place? Would you like a drink?

MAUREEN. Port and lemon please.

COMPÈRE. Shall I tell you who drinks that? Mick Jagger. It's true. (*He and* JULIE *go through the door*.) Bacardi and Coke for you, isn't it, Julie?

JULIE. I'm surprised you remember — it's over a week ago.

COMPÈRE (*getting hold of her*). You made quite an impression on me.

JULIE. Did I?

COMPÈRE. I want to have a little talk with you. What do you think you're doing here tonight.

JULIE. I'm singing in a Talent Contest.

COMPÈRE. And do you think you'll win?

JULIE. I don't know.

COMPÈRE. Well, I'll tell you something — you won't win. Jacky James's manager runs this club, and he wants Jacky to do the Bunter's circuit — it's money in both their pockets.

JULIE. Oh well, it doesn't really matter.

COMPÈRE. Even if you won, your prospects aren't that bright.

You say you're twenty-four, you may be more, I don't know. You've got a mediocre voice, a terrible Lancashire accent, no experience and no act. On your own, you're going to get nowhere fast. But with me — I know more big producers than you've had hot dinners. A word from me, and you could do a guest spot on the Des O'Connor Show, Stars on Sunday — there's plenty of people willing to do me a favour. Hughie Green's got a new show coming up soon — want me to put in a word for you?

JULIE. That would be really nice of you.

COMPÈRE. I didn't say I would, but I might. (*Puts his arm around her.*) You're a very attractive girl, Julie, I'm sure I'm not the first to tell you that?

JULIE. No.

COMPÈRE. And that's a very nice dress. I like it. But I'd like it more if it was lying on a heap on my bedroom carpet. (*Puts her hand on his crotch.*) You can feel how excited you've made me. Now, tonight's out, unfortunately. But my wife's away tomorrow, brass rubbing. I don't think you'll be disappointed. I flatter myself I could give you a reasonable time. Nobody's complained yet, anyway, and old John Thomas has put a smile on a lot of girls' faces — famous ones as well. (*Looks at his watch.*) The Grill Room's over there. Think about it.

JULIE *rushes off. The* COMPÈRE *goes back into the room.*

They haven't got any port, darling. I came back to see what you wanted instead.

MAUREEN. That's very kind of you — most men would bring you half a bitter or something, and expect you to like it.

COMPÈRE. I flatter myself I'm not like most men. Cigarette? I'm sorry, I don't know your name.

MAUREEN. Maureen. Not very exciting.

COMPÈRE. It's a lovely name. It suits you. Irish, isn't it?

MAUREEN. I don't know. I think there is a little bit of Irish on my mother's side.

COMPÈRE. Well, you've certainly got those lovely Irish blue eyes — very striking.

MAUREEN. I've always thought they were more of a blue-grey. Like my hair — it's not really blonde, and it's not really light brown. I suppose the word's mousey.

COMPÈRE (*stroking it*). Whatever the colour, it's beautifully soft. Smells nice, too.

MAUREEN. Strawberry and melon shampoo, for fine flyaway hair. But there's a bit of perfume on it too. Kiku.

COMPÈRE. It's very sexy. Have you got a boyfriend, Maureen?

MAUREEN. No, not at the moment. I've just chucked one, actually.

COMPÈRE. I'm very lucky, aren't I?

MAUREEN. Sorry?

COMPÈRE. To catch you between boyfriends. I'm sure that doesn't happen very often.

MAUREEN. No.

COMPÈRE. How old do you think I am?

MAUREEN. Thirty-five?

COMPÈRE. Well — not far out. Still a lot older than you.

MAUREEN. It doesn't matter really these days. I mean, Hayley Mills . . .

COMPÈRE. The thing about an older man — you find he knows what's really attractive. He isn't taken in by silly little girls like your friend Julie.

MAUREEN. Don't you think she's pretty?

COMPÈRE. What's pretty? I'm talking about sex.

MAUREEN. Oh.

COMPÈRE. I know what I'm talking about. I was in the Black and White Minstrels for seven and a half years. Now, the girls in the show were pretty enough, but they didn't excite me in the slightest.

MAUREEN. What's Dai Francis like?

COMPÈRE (*puts her hand on his trousers*). Now, you can feel how excited you've made me.

MAUREEN *moves her hand away quickly.*

You're a nice big girl, aren't you, Maureen?

MAUREEN. Well, a bit too big, I think.

COMPÈRE. No, it's lovely. I bet you're wonderful in bed. The sort of body a man could lose himself in.

MAUREEN. I've never had any complaints.

COMPÈRE. I bet you haven't. I bet you've got lovely big nipples, as well, haven't you?

MAUREEN. Well — medium big.

COMPÈRE. Well, look, I'm a bit tied up now, obviously — got to go and sort out this farcical Talent Contest. Honestly, these fumbling magicians and tone-deaf singers just about send me up the wall. But after it's over, you nip out to my car — it's in the private car park on the left as you come in. It's the white Cortina against the wall. I'll meet you there, and we can have twenty minutes or so before I go back. OK? (*He starts to leave by stage door.*) And if you've got a pantie girdle on or anything like that — take it off, eh? They're bloody murder to deal with in the back seat of a car, and we won't have much time. And bring a tissue. (*He leaves.*)

MAUREEN *looks down her dress, trying to gauge the size of her nipples. She takes a breath spray from her bag, and uses it. She riffles through her make-up, sees a tissue, smoothes it, folds it, and puts it back.* JULIE *opens the door a crack.*

JULIE. Maur! Where's that compère?

MAUREEN. He's round the other side. (*She goes to the stage door*) He's announcing that magician, you'll be on in a minute.

JULIE. Oh, Jesus, give us a cigarette. Oh bloody hell.

MAUREEN. What's up?

JULIE. I can't do this, you know.

MAUREEN. Course you can.

JULIE. 'Course you can, Malcolm.'

MAUREEN. What?

JULIE. You know, 'Oh, Mub, I can't take my exams blocked up like this' . . . I can't go on and sing, you know.

MAUREEN. Look, it's only stage fright — you'll be all right when you get on there. I was the same when I was a courtier in *As You Like It* at school — just stage fright.

JULIE. It's not. It's Mel, the bloody organist.

MAUREEN. Why, what's the matter?

JULIE. He can't play — that's what's the matter. He's like bloody Les Dawson. Honestly, what a nit. You know there's a bit before you start singing: (*Sings a few bars.*) then I start. Well, he said we don't need to bother with that — I'll come in when you do. So I'm looking at him, and he's looking at me — in the end he says, why don't you start. I said, I don't know what bloody note it is, do I? So he said, I'll play your note four times in rhythm. That sounded wonderful, as you can imagine — it was like my Nan's clock. We went through it anyway — it was diabolical. Sometimes he was really slow, and other times he was about eight words ahead of me. So I said, Thank you very much, I've got to put my clean knickers on now, and pissed off. God, what a twat. I'm bloody glad he never married me, now. I thought Dave was bad enough.

MAUREEN. It might be all right when you come to do it — now that you've run it through.

JULIE. I doubt it. He had about half a bottle of whisky just in the time I was there. And his wife! She's got a permanent job here. I thought she'd be really good. She was singing a song when I went in. She sounded like that mad woman that gets up at closing time in the Britannia. And she looked like God, I don't know what — that Muppet that dances round with the long blonde hair and a mouth like this. (*She mimes an inane grin.*) She's welcome to Mel, I know that much. I can't go on, anyway.

MAUREEN. That's daft — you might win — all those other clubs at £50 a night.

JULIE. Well, for one, I won't win. And for two, if they're all like this tatty dump, I'd rather stay at home laughing at people on *Opportunity Knocks*.

JULIE *sings 'Bored With This'*:

Bored With This

I'm bored with this
It's a stupid game
Things look good
But they're all the same
I'll be back in the office
Monday morning
Yawning 'Morning,
Morning, morning.'

What you missed
Russell Harty
Save my talents
For the office party
I'm going to hand in my notice
I think
Hello Dave
Hello sink.

Get an office leaving present
I'm supposed to weep
Something bloody useless
Something cheap
'Don't get anything
We know she likes,
Get a stainless steel meat platter
With spikes.'

Up the aisle in white
Well you have to don't you?
Honeymoon Corfu
You will write won't you?
Going away outfit

Blue with pink accessories
Matching lightweight cases
Full of Dutch caps and pessaries.

Have the boss to dinner
Help my husband's job
I'll be dead inventive
With corn on the cob.
And in nine months' time
You never know
I might win a squashed tomato
In a Baby-gro

Do keep-fit
On Tuesday nights
Crimplene cardie
Footless tights;
Or Cordon Bleu —
Can you see me — 'Sorry
I thought Coq au Vin
Was a fuck in a lorry.'

And at forty five
No doubt
I'll be winking at the milkman
When my womb's dropped out
Too much make-up
Double chin
Watching *Jackanory*
With a bottle of gin.

Stuffed with Valium,
Nicotine, caffeine
You never know
I might die laughing.

MAUREEN. You don't know you won't win.

JULIE. I do. It's fixed. Jacky James is going to win. But I could be on Stars on Sunday (*Creases up laughing.*) if . . . Oh, God.

MAUREEN. What?

JULIE. If I have it off with that compère tomorrow night.

MAUREEN. What?

JULIE. Just before I went in to practise my song, he took me on one side. He said he'd get me on TV if I had it off with him, and he's all staring down my dress and everything. And then — he put my hand on his trousers, and said 'you can feel how excited you've made me!' And I'm trying to keep a straight face. I'll have to wash my hands.

Both laughing more and more.

MAUREEN. He did that to me, as well.

JULIE. What?

MAUREEN. Put my hand on his . . .

JULIE. He didn't! Oh no, the dirty old sod. What else did he do?

MAUREEN. He said, did I have big nipples?

JULIE. Oh no! You should have said — bigger than your cock, mate. Honestly, when he put my hand on it, I'm thinking — where is it, and what's he doing with a packet of Polos in his underpants.

MAUREEN. He asked me to meet him by his car after, and take my pantie girdle off.

JULIE. What a creep. Come on, we're going!

JULIE starts to gather up her things.

MAUREEN. Someone'll see us.

JULIE. No, they won't — there's a fire escape thing near the Henry VIII Grill. Hurry up before he comes to find me. Pantie girdle! I'm surprised he didn't say bloomers and liberty bodice. He's got a nerve. He must be about fifty-five.

MAUREEN. I know, I thought that.

JULIE. Now, have we got everything?

MAUREEN. Yes, except your hat-full.

JULIE. I'll leave that for a present. Are you all right?

MAUREEN. Yes.

JULIE (*does elaborate sneaking-across-room acting*). I'm Starsky and Hutch, me. (*As they leave.*) Hey, it's not all that late, you know. That cinema near the station's got dirty films on. My Swedish Meatball.

MAUREEN. What's that about?

JULIE. School dinners. Honestly. Maureen. Hey, don't forget your pantie girdle.

They leave. ARTHUR *and* GEORGE *come in from the stage door. Faint sounds of applause.*

ARTHUR. They certainly liked that, George.

GEORGE. They didn't throw anything.

ARTHUR. Are you not doing banjo finale?

GEORGE. Aye, go on, I don't mind.

Picks up his banjo and goes back on stage. ARTHUR *sits down, and begins to practise the six card repeat.*

Good Fun

Good Fun was first performed at the Crucible Theatre, Sheffield, in April 1980 with the following cast:

LIZ, *community arts administrator, 24,*	Annabel Leventon
FRANK, *librarian, 28,*	Charles McKeown
MIKE, *geography teacher, 30,*	Gregory Floy
ELSIE, *bistro barmaid, 24,*	Victoria Wood
LYNNE, *on Job Creation, speaks with a strong Lancashire accent, 19,*	Sue Wallace
KEV, *unemployed, remedial Lancashire accent, 19,*	Joe Figg
BETTY, *cosmetics saleswoman, concealed Lancashire accent, 52,*	Julie Walters
GAIL, *domestic science teacher, dreary Lancashire accent, 24,*	Noreen Kershaw
MAURICE, *head of Co-op carpet department, 53,*	Christopher Hancock

Directed by David Leland
Musical Director David Firman

Good Fun was again performed at the Crucible Theatre, Sheffield, in June 1980 with the following cast changes:

LIZ	Polly James
FRANK	Sam Kelly
BETTY	Meg Johnson

Time
This summer.

Set

The annexe of an Arts Centre in the North West of England. It is the top floor of an old neglected building, such as a church hall, infant school or Conservative Club.

It is all one large room, but at one side is an office, separated by some kind of partition — so that someone in the office would not necessarily be visible to someone in the main space. Access to the room is through the office, and there is another door at the other end marked 'Toilet'.

The main space has in it a small platform with an old piano on it, a kitchen area with sink, cooker, cupboards, table and chairs.

The rest of the space is full of cardboard boxes, old spotlights, tins of paint, bundles of stage curtains, etc. The whole place is dirty and bare, and painted in institutional colours.

ACT ONE

LIZ is in the office. She sings her song. During the musical break after 'the pain cannot be seen', the bell rings, she picks up the phone, presses the buzzer, and carries on singing.

At the end of the song, FRANK comes in, and attempts to tickle her.

LIZ (*sings*)

Liz's Song

I'm the one the play's about
Just want to introduce myself
And put my side of things before we start.
I'm Liz and I'm the heroine
I'm friendly and outgoing
I've got 'A' levels in scripture, maths and art.

I'm not exactly Joni Mitchell
Good old Lizzie, pints of bitter
Army overcoats and not a hint of sex,
With a body like a drawing by a student in a life class
Who was sitting at the back without his specs.

I'm really nearly always busy
Always something that needs doing
But the days have cracks-thoughts force themselves between
Love-why do you think nobody loves me
When I'm nice and kind, it's very odd
I feel like those smiling people who try to hand
     you leaflets about God
Do you know what I mean?
Love – I'm so loving it's pathetic

I'll run your life or run you to the shops
I feel like I'm playing pass the parcel but the
    music never stops
Do you know what I mean?
Still you keep on smiling so the pain cannot be
    seen.

I live alone, I'm not a couple
I can't justify the purchase
Of my deep-dyed double-fitted bottom sheet
So I don't have milk delivered
I make tea with just one tea bag
Takes me months to finish up the Shredded Wheat.
When the party gets exciting
And the inhibitions vanish
And the music sends the dancers into frenzies
You will find me in the corner
Mopping sick and washing ashtrays
Helping drunk fiancés find their contact lenses.

Always something that needs doing
But the days have cracks — thoughts force themselves
    between
Love — though I always ask directions
I seem to be continually misled
I feel like I'm trying to get to Euston but I've
    lost my *A to Z*
Do you know what I mean?
Love — why does no one I want want me —
You see a friend whose face lights up your night
You smile they cross the room towards the person
    on your right
Do you know what I mean?
Still you keep on smiling so the pain cannot be seen.

Buzzer.

I am not without admirers-
Buck-teethed amateur saxophonists in
Green acrylic cardigans are game
They give lifts in their three wheelers

And glimpses of string underpants
And whisper Django Reinhart's middle name.

But tonight it's a librarian
Delivered by caesarian
So mummy dear could keep her ankles crossed-
Impervious to hint or snub
Thinks a clitoris is a flowering shrub
And I'm too nice to tell him to get lost.

Get lost, Frank.

FRANK. You're only saying that because you mean it, Ha ha.

LIZ *ignores him, and carries on with what she was doing,
which wasn't a lot. Pause.*

FRANK. Good news about the Pollen Count. (*Cracks his
knuckles.*)

LIZ. Stop doing that.

FRANK. Sorry. (*Does it again.*) Sorry. You're looking awfully
pretty today. What is that stuff? Butter muslin?

LIZ (*for the twenty-fifth time*). Cheesecloth.

FRANK. Right idea, wrong dairy process. Look, I didn't come
round here just to be funny. (*Fumbling in pocket.*) Now, just
once in a while, I can be reasonably impulsive — what do you
think these are? (*Waving keys in her face.*)

LIZ. The keys for your moped padlock.

FRANK. Ah, yes. Quite right. Sorry. (*Fetches out another set
of keys.*) How do you fancy packing a few skirts and coming
with me to my Auntie Ida's luxury caravan outside Aberystwyth?

LIZ. A dirty weekend?

FRANK. Well, Auntie Ida would be there too. She's lent me the
spare keys in case she gets mugged on her way to the
washblock. How about it?

LIZ. I can't, I've got someone coming to stay.

FRANK. Which gender? Slender tender gender, or . . . (*Runs out
of inspiration.*) a man?

LIZ. It's Elsie. I've not seen her since I met Mike; I just fancy a quiet weekend lounging around chatting about my emotional development. Actually I really feel the need to discuss things properly with a woman.

FRANK. Can't you discuss them with me? Oh, a woman — sorry. 'See you after the operation.'

LIZ. What operation?

FRANK. It's something comedians say. On the television. 'And now he's had the operation.' It isn't me that's particularly fond of variety, but my mother likes magicians. Someone showed her something when she was five, she's never forgotten it. Is Elsie like you? I shall be jolly keen on her if she is.

LIZ. Quite like me; she's not as enlightened, and her tits are bigger.

FRANK. I think your . . . you knows are rather something. I told my mother you didn't wear a — didn't like the, er, fettered aspect.

LIZ. What did she say?

FRANK. She said I'd probably got it wrong, and you probably wore one of the new sort without the wires in. (*Taking out crumpled chocolate cake made from Rice Krispies.*) I saved this for you from my lunch. It's been there all day, so it's a bit warm. My mother made it.

LIZ. No thanks, I've given up chocolate, it's a stimulant.

FRANK. Gosh, is it? Doesn't seem to have worked on Mother yet. (*Looming in.*) I say, it's her Home of Compassion night tonight, so I'm not in a hurry.

LIZ. What about your tea?

FRANK. She said I could spend my Kentucky Fried Chicken voucher, as long as I ate it in the kitchen with the extractor fan on. I could fetch some, and bring it back here. We could both have some, and lick each other's fingers. (*Looms in.*) I do things I shouldn't in the night, when I think of you. I've cut your photo out of the North West Arts *Monthly Bulletin.* I've had to change my pyjamas twice this week.

LIZ. Oh, spare me the details.

FRANK. I've got the right equipment.

LIZ. I should hope so. Get off.

FRANK. I mean precaution-wise. I went to an unfamiliar Boots. Three dozen. Should see us through till January 1984, which is when they perish.

The doorbell rings. LIZ *answers it.*

LIZ. Hi . . . Oh, nobody important. You know you can come up any time, Mike; I'm here to help. (*Knees* FRANK *in the balls.*) Sure, come up. (*Presses button.*)

FRANK. I say, watch it. I jolly nearly could have hurt myself a little bit then. It's a good job I usually have a Penguin down there.

LIZ. Look, Mike's coming up.

FRANK. That's still going on, is it?

LIZ. I need to be alone with him for a bit. Can you go in the toilet?

FRANK. All right. What shall I do, though?

LIZ. You could start some more papier mâché.

FRANK. All right. Where are the newspapers?

LIZ. I think we used them all. (*Seeing pile of old scripts.*) Oh, use these. (*Pushing him towards the door.*)

FRANK. Are you sure? These are playscripts, aren't they?

LIZ. Yes, but they're unsolicited.

FRANK *goes into the toilet.* LIZ *does hasty hair-patting, liplicking and musk-oil applying.* MIKE *comes in.*

Hi.

MIKE *sits down, not looking at her.*

Whisky? (*Pause.*) I know it floods the system with toxins, but you need a few toxins by Friday afternoon. (*Pours them one each.*) I'm really sorry about yesterday. I'll try not to ask so many questions. Just bring the car back when you want to. (*Pause*.) How's the flat?

MIKE. OK.

LIZ. Well, just let me know when you want me to come round and clean it again.

MIKE. No, I've sussed it out — that's why people have nervous breakdowns.

LIZ. Why?

MIKE. Because they don't breathe in enough dust. They suck it up with machines and throw it away. It's all wrong. We need it. It's earth, right? Powdered earth. It clears your head out like bran clears your bowels out.

LIZ. Really? Yes, I can see that. I'm surprised I never thought of it myself.

MIKE. You see, I was looking at the vacuum cleaner, right? I'd been smoking, and suddenly, I didn't know what it was.

LIZ. Go on.

MIKE. I couldn't cope with it. A machine that sucks up the earth. Terrifying. Had to get it out.

LIZ. My Hoover?

MIKE. Thought it was going to suck me up. I threw it through the window.

LIZ. That's fine.

MIKE. You can see incredible things through a broken window. Everybody's house should have a wall missing. Then you'd really see people for what they were — ants, worms, mindless. Have you got your cheque book?

LIZ. How's it going?

MIKE. What?

LIZ. What my mother would call a commune.

MIKE. What would you call it?

LIZ. I suppose I'd call it a commune too.

MIKE. Well, we should have the first tepees set up any day now.

LIZ. Great. I wish I could be there. (*Hands over cheque.*) There you go.

MIKE. Cheers. I'm not into bread or anything, but once this Punch and Judy thing gets off the ground, I'll pay you back.

LIZ. Oh, don't worry, it's a privilege to be involved. Oh, the booth came. (*Indicates large bundle of bamboo, striped canvas, etc.*)

MIKE. Amazing.

LIZ. Actually, I was thinking, you have got the first show coming up quite soon, maybe we should get a little bit of work done.

MIKE. No hurry. I've got a new angle on it, actually.

LIZ. It's just that it'll be quite a big show, and I've been telling everybody about my new discovery — an avant-garde Punch and Judy man, I've given you quite a build-up. I was wondering if we shouldn't start writing the script, or something.

MIKE. It's the crocodile.

LIZ. Yes?

MIKE. Make the crocodile the Department of Health and Social Security, and the whole thing falls into place.

LIZ. That's amazing.

MIKE. No, it's not — you think about it.

LIZ. Mm, you're right, it's not. Frank, look, I've got Frank started on the papier mâché. Perhaps you could model the crocodile, or perhaps Frank should have a go?

FRANK *comes into the office.*

FRANK. Eh what sorry pardon? Earhole dicky, dicky earhole.

LIZ. Do you think you could start modelling a crocodile? You saw how I did Punch and Judy.

FRANK. Well, it's only my first plunge into papier mâché. I've never been very artistic.

MIKE. I've got a theory about the hangman too.

FRANK. Though, I must admit I have a seminal memory of raffia.

LIZ. Do you know what seminal means?

FRANK. I think you'll find I do, yes.

LIZ. It's to do with semen.

FRANK. My watch is still working, three cheers for Ingersoll. (*Hovers.*) Polycell then. (*Leaps away.*)

MIKE (*shouting*). I'm trying to tell you about the bloody hangman!

LIZ. Sorry. Go on.

Doorbell rings.

Hang on.

MIKE. Leave it.

LIZ. I'm expecting someone.

MIKE. I don't want to see anybody.

Doorbell rings.

LIZ. It's probably Elsie.

FRANK *leaps in.*

FRANK. Shall I? Jolly James Bond, this, isn't it? Hello, Annary Grannexe, Granary Annexe, Elizabeth Marshall's office speaking. Hold on please. Someone looking for the Noddy and Big Ears sex clinic — is that over the road?

LIZ. It's Elsie. Let her in (*To* MIKE:) Do you mind?

MIKE. I don't think I'll stay. I can't face absorbing a new aura.

LIZ. Oh. You could tell her about the tepees. I'm sure she'll be really interested.

MIKE. Maybe.

FRANK. That was a joke then, was it?

LIZ. What?

FRANK. About Noddy and Big Ears.

LIZ. Frank, go and put the kettle on. (*She exits.*)

ELSIE (*entering*). I'm looking for Liz, is she here?

MIKE. Is anybody really here? Are you here? Frightening isn't it?

Pause.

ELSIE (*to* FRANK). Is Liz around?

FRANK. A round what? Ha ha. (ELSIE *bangs her head against the wall.*) Sorry, typical Friday behaviour for me, I'm afraid. Liz is in the, it's rather awkward to flush. You have to pull the chain in a certain rhythm. (*Pause.*) It's the first three notes of *Hava Nagila*, if you have to pay a visit. I expect Liz told you about my fiasco with the xerox money?

ELSIE. No.

FRANK. I still get ribbed about it, and it happened last November. What vitamins do you get from honey?

ELSIE. I don't know.

FRANK. B.

ELSIE. Really.

FRANK. B double E, I mean. Bzz.

LIZ *comes out of the toilet.*

LIZ. Hi. Lovely to see you. Good journey?

ELSIE. Well —

LIZ. Great. Look, come and meet my emotional investment. Mike, this is Elsie.

MIKE. You can't cope with confrontations can you?

ELSIE. Yes.

FRANK. Frank. How do you do?

ELSIE. How do you do?

FRANK. How do you do? Oh sorry, shouldn't have shaken hands with you because of my wart.

ELSIE. That's OK. (*Pretending to be sick.*)

LIZ. Make the tea, Frank. Tea?

ELSIE. Anything. I stopped at the Services but the woman on the tea urn had impetigo so I just had the sugar lumps. Only Gail hasn't come has she?

LIZ. No she never even answered the letter.

ELSIE. P'raps she sussed it out.

LIZ. I don't see why, this is just the sort of place they hold those reunions.

ELSIE. Is this where you've been promoted to?

LIZ. Yes. Good, isn't it? I'm in charge of everything that goes on in here.

ELSIE. So, what does?

LIZ. Well, you see, basically it's an adaptable space; that is, a space that can be adapted, adapted for the particular use of the particular people who are using the space.

ELSIE. For instance?

LIZ. For instance, if they need some kind of stage, they can use the stage, if they want to use the floor, they can use the floor . . .

ELSIE. And if they want to use the ceiling, they'll have to have suckers on their feet.

LIZ. Yeah.

MIKE. Have you ever looked at bread? I mean really looked at it?

ELSIE. I got poked in the eye with a French loaf once.

MIKE (*leaving*). I'll come back when your friend lets her defences down a bit. It's not good to be so hostile, it's not good. (*He leaves.*)

LIZ. Oh dear (*Pause.*) Don't blame yourself. (*Pause.*) Try and relax.

ELSIE. I am relaxed.

LIZ. He's a bit sensitive at the moment, he's got a big show coming up soon. You see, Mike's an avant-garde Punch and Judy man and he's the star of my first big thing in the Annexe.

ELSIE. What is it?

LIZ. Have you got a programme, Frank? I've left mine somewhere.

FRANK (*whipping one out of top pocket*). Abracadabra, as they say on the television. It's not me that's particularly fond of variety . . .

LIZ. Frank.

FRANK. Sorry.

ELSIE (*reading from the back of the leaflet*). 'To ward off an attack, squat over a washing-up bowl full of warm water and sea-salt.' Oh, to ward off an attack of cystitis.

LIZ. This show I'm doing is for their Annual Rally. All the cystitis sufferers.

ELSIE. Like Alcoholics Anonymous? My name is Elsie and I wee a lot?

LIZ. They're meeting in the park, having speeches.

FRANK *is very busy with his papier mâché, very messily.*

ELSIE. It'll be difficult to hold the attention of the crowd, won't it? People nipping behind the rhodies every five minutes.

LIZ. They'll have megaphones.

ELSIE. Oh, to speak through.

LIZ. And then they're marching to the annexe, that's here, and I'm laying on this huge party for them — disco, booze, Punch and Judy . . . I must do something about it soon.

FRANK. Yes, when is it exactly.

LIZ. Oh, not for ages.

ELSIE. According to this, it's tomorrow.

LIZ. No, it isn't.

ELSIE. It is.

LIZ. Oh dear, I didn't realise it was tomorrow.

ELSIE. And you haven't done anything about it?

LIZ. I've had the leaflets printed. I just hadn't booked any of the people. Oh well, I'll just have to send myself a telegram and call myself away again. They're costing me a fortune these telegrams.

FRANK. Biddy wasn't convinced about the last one.

ELSIE. Who's Biddy?

LIZ. She's my boss. Fifteen stone of lentil-stained kaftan. She'd go bonkers about this, thank Christ she's on holiday.

FRANK. She came back this morning.

LIZ. Oh no.

FRANK. Don't worry. She was probably joking when she said she could have you fired for incompetence.

LIZ. Did she really say that?

FRANK. Oh yes. Twice.

LIZ. Oh shit. What am I going to do?

ELSIE. Tell her you've blown it. She can't be that bad.

LIZ. No? She's into battered wives. If there aren't any around she has some battered.

ELSIE. Tell her someone in your family's just died.

LIZ. I'm always telling her that. She's started calling me Rose Kennedy. I daren't tell Biddy.

ELSIE. Well she's going to find out. It's going to get round when 300 cystitis sufferers burst in and find there's no party and the toilet only flushes to the first three notes of *Hava Nagila*.

LIZ. OK. Then we may as well go now. Frank — you pack me the kettle and all my clothes. Elsie you get my afghan and my sleeping-bag.

ELSIE. Back on the dole on Monday then, eh? Good job they wouldn't let you have a mortgage for that derelict abbatoir in Salford.

LIZ. Ah.

ELSIE. What's up?

LIZ. Well I'm sure Mike won't mind, but he's setting up a commune in North Wales, and they're buying this field and I'm paying the mortgage, a bit.

MIKE *returns.*

MIKE. What's the problem?

LIZ. Nothing, it's just that Frank forgot to tell me the Rally was tomorrow so I'm going to have to cancel it, and leave, and sign on, and it might be a bit impossible for me to manage the repayments for a few weeks is that OK.?

MIKE. Yes, that's fine. It was a nice idea, getting up a community where people could live in love and friendship, in tune with the rhythms of the earth, I've had a really good time planning it for three years. Still, you have to be open to change. Don't feel bad about it, this has happened because you've made it happen. There's no need to feel guilty just because you're not strong enough to make a real commitment. See you.

LIZ. Don't go, please. I'm sure we can work something out, can't we, Elsie?

ELSIE. Eh?

LIZ. We'll have to do it.

ELSIE. What?

LIZ. The party — we'll have to fix it up.

ELSIE. Food and drink and an evening's entertainment by tomorrow afternoon?

LIZ. Yes, good heavens, it won't be that difficult. It's not as if it has to be really good — they're only cystitis sufferers aren't they? Yes, come on, we'll all muck in together. I mean, it's good fun, really in a way isn't it?

She sings:

Community Arts

English girls enjoy a crisis
English girls don't fall to bits
I think I'm the sort of girl who would have really
    loved the Blitz.

> Come on, let's rise to the occasion
> We can make this party work
> Let's not forget I have relations
> One of whom was at Dunkirk.
> Though we're batting on a sticky wicket
> I can save the day,
> And then my grateful friends will turn to me and say:

FRANK (*rises, sings*).

> If Liz is fighting the battle
> We can't help but win
> You're our air-raid shelter, you're our Vera Lynn
> And she's our Lancaster bomber, our Spitfire as
>   well
> You're Monty, you're Itma, you're Alvar Liddell
> So we can march on to Victory with joy in our hearts
> You're the Churchill of Community Arts.

LIZ. What's up, Elsie?

ELSIE. I just think you have as much chance of pulling it off as the band on the Titanic had of getting an encore.

LIZ. But we've always helped each other out before. You did my algebra, I ate your swedes.

ELSIE. All right, I'll try and help you sort it out.

LIZ. I mean, luckily, I know a hell of a lot of people in this business. I only need to pick up the phone and this room will be swarming with Morris Dancers.

> There are countless women's theatre groups
> That I can call on any time
> Recorder Consorts, left-wing cellists,

FRANK. Friends who've done a bit of mime.

LIZ. All I need now is my dialling finger, our
>   problems will be gone

ELSIE. As Britain's star performers all reply as one:

FRANK. If Liz is booking the show

ELSIE. Then we've got to be there

LIZ. Would you ignore Sinatra,

ELSIE. Turn down Fred Astaire.

FRANK. Refuse employment with Gielgud.

ELSIE \
FRANK } What we're saying is:
We'd crawl halfway up a mountain just to work
　　　with Liz.

LIZ \
ELSIE } So we'll be tying our bells on, and learning
　　our parts

ELSIE \
FRANK } For the Lew Grade of Community Arts.

LIZ. Mike — it could be everything we've ever talked about —
your Punch and Judy, your worm paintings, we could set up
stalls and sell those necklaces you made out of —

MIKE. Tampons, yeah.

LIZ. And we could use all the recipes in your book: 137 things
to do with Bran. But honestly, I don't want to do it without
you because anybody can throw a party but if you're involved
it becomes a disturbingly, creative, artistic experience.

MIKE. True. And who am I to deprive you of that?

LIZ. And when the music stops and the party's over

ELSIE. Empty plate and cup,

MIKE. The guests will turn and say

ALL FOUR. We'll do the washing-up —

FRANK \
ELSIE } 'Cos we can't thank you enough
MIKE / We'll just say with a smile

MIKE. You've made having cystitis completely worthwhile

ALL FOUR. You made this tatty old room seem like the Albert
　　　　　　Hall
We had more than a party, we had a ball
We're full of music and laughter and

MIKE. Wholemeal Bakewell Tart

FRANK. } You've surmounted disaster, time never passed faster,
MIKE   }

FRANK. Lady Astor

ALL FOUR. Of Community Arts.

LIZ. Off we go then, let's all just chuck in suggestions to start
with. Mike?

MIKE. I think what would be really good; if we cleared the whole
space out, sprayed it all over in gold, then laid one perfect turd
in the middle of the floor.

Pause.

LIZ. Mmm, incredible. Elsie?

ELSIE. I don't think we should do that.

LIZ. Frank?

FRANK. The main thing is to organise the thing.

LIZ. Wonderful Frank. Go on.

FRANK. Now, if I bring my four-colour biro in on this, and these
brand-new 5" by 3" filing cards. (*Everyone is waiting for
something good.*) Now, I'll divide each card into two, with my
ruler. I'll just do the first one, as an example, I can finish the
rest later. (*Rules a line down the middle of the card.*) Now in
this column, in red, I'm going to write '47 pence'. Well, 'p',
to save ink, '47p'.

LIZ. What for?

FRANK. That's the price of the filing cards you owe me. Now, in
the other column, in blue, we need to put . . .

LIZ. Oh, shut up, Frank, we're trying to organise a party — fun,
laughter, music.

Pause.

ELSIE. Look, shall I go out and get some booze and something
to eat. How much money have you got?

LIZ. Well, sort of, not a lot, not any, really. But we're OK. for
food because there's plenty of stuff here. I can get Lynne over
from the Salad Bar to make something, and we can heat it up

tomorrow. (*Goes over to food cupboard.*) Oh, yes. I'm sure there's something wonderful you can do with oats.

ELSIE. How about booze?

LIZ. No problem. Frank — get that parsnip wine out of the toilet? (*He gets it.*) It's not actually supposed to mature until 1982, but we can mix it with (*Looks in cupboard.*) — rosehip syrup. Fine — punch — nice. Just put a few apples in it. Are those cloves?

ELSIE. No, they're carpet tacks.

FRANK *brings wine,* ELSIE *tastes it.*

LIZ. What do you think?

ELSIE. It's horrible. (*Picks up a glass of painting water from the same table and sips it.*) What's this?

LIZ. Painting water

ELSIE. It's nice.

LIZ. Now, we've got the Punch and Judy.

ELSIE. Have we? That's all fixed, is it?

LIZ. Oh yes, if someone can find out how to put the booth up, and finish the puppets, while I write the script. So Mike and I will get on with that now. Party Games! There's that one where someone goes out of the room . . .

ELSIE. And the other people criticize their jumper. It's called working in an office.

LIZ (*getting out booth*). Here's a nice job, Frank. Putting this up. Now, it's quite simple. The instructions are in Japanese, but all the sticks are numbered, and there should be a diagram — there was a diagram. Anyway, the man in the shop said it practically puts itself up.

ELSIE *and* FRANK *look at it.*

Gosh, I'm exhausted. Now, Punch and Judy. (*Sits down next to* MIKE.) What we said yesterday was, Judy's pregnant, because of faulty counselling by the Family Planning.

ELSIE. It says 'barbecue' on here.

LIZ. Can you ring the Freezer Centre for me? (*Writes some numbers down.*) We could order part of a pig.

ELSIE. Which part?

LIZ. You could pick it up tomorrow.

ELSIE. It says TV personalities here.

LIZ (*writing down another number*). There's an agency I've used before. I set up this thing where you could throw custard pies at people from Radio 4.

ELSIE (*dialling a number*). There's not going to be anyone in now, is there?

LIZ. They're open till eight on Fridays.

ELSIE. What shall I say?

LIZ. Find out how much it costs first. (*She is not paying much attention, trying to write her script.*)

ELSIE. Hello, I wonder if you could tell me how much you charge for a television personality to make a personal appearance at a party — a sort of Radio 4-type person, or the men that stand at the back in *That's Life*. (*Pause.*) Thank you. (*Puts phone down.*)

LIZ. Well?

ELSIE. That was the Freezer Centre. They didn't know.

LIZ. That 834 number's the agency. But there won't be anybody there now. (*Gets out phone book.*) Ring Granada.

ELSIE. Eh?

LIZ. Well, there might be somebody off *Coronation Street* hanging around in the bar, someone who could nip over for a few minutes tomorrow. Here you are.

ELSIE. Who shall I ask for? I mean, who do you want? Ena Sharples? (*Dialling.*)

LIZ. No, she'll be really expensive. One of the smaller parts. I don't know, I never watch it.

ELSIE. Oh, come on, you were practically on Librium when Ernie Bishop got shot. It's ringing.

LIZ. Ask for the bar.

ELSIE. Hello, could you put me through to the bar, please? Oh, can you hang on a minute? They haven't got a bar.

LIZ. Canteen.

ELSIE. Can you put me through to the canteen, then? — It's shut. Well, look, I'm sorry to bother you, but there aren't any people from *Coronation Street* hanging about, are there? Not Elsie Tanner or somebody, a smaller sort of person — yeah, him, or her. No, he was shot, don't you remember? . . . Thanks a lot, anyway . . . Bye. There's nobody there, and they don't come in on Saturdays.

LIZ. Well, look, look in the *Yellow Pages*, I must get on with this script.

ELSIE. What under, TV personalities?

LIZ (*going back to* MIKE). Entertainers, anybody, groups, musicians . . .

   Pause.

MIKE. Or maybe I should be the puppet and Punch is twenty-feet high and working me.

LIZ. Great. Now, what do you think, Mike? Are they going to know the wine-gum is a Dutch cap?

ELSIE. Can I speak to Billy Banana, please? Is that Mrs Banana? I was wondering if your husband was free to do a party tomorrow night? . . . No, it's grown-ups — cystitis sufferers . . . No, I wouldn't feel like a party, if I had it . . . No, I've never had that, I don't wear them, no, I didn't know it stopped you giving blood. OK. — she's gone to fetch the book, see if he's free.

LIZ. Find out how much he is.

ELSIE. Hello, oh, is he? Great. Can you tell me how much he charges? Thanks, just hold on, can you? It's £50 for twenty minutes, and £100 if he brings his exploding moped.

LIZ. I can't afford it.

ELSIE. I'm afraid that's a bit more than we wanted to pay . . .
Hold on . . . £25 and he'll parade around your garden, pulling
ping-pong balls out of people's ears. Ten quid, and he sits in
your living-room and gets on your nerves. I'm sorry, can I
ring you back tomorrow, and perhaps fix something up, if
he's still free? Thanks a lot. Bye.

LIZ. Look under musicians. (*To* MIKE:) I haven't got time to
paint a set of the Chiswick Women's Aid, let alone model
Erin Pizzey out of papier mâché.

ELSIE. Nothing — two piano teachers and the Glen Miller Style
Radcliffe All-Star Big Band.

LIZ. We can't afford them. Any comedians?

ELSIE. There's a few coal-merchants, shall I see if they know any
jokes?

LIZ. Oh, forget it, there's plenty of time, we can work something
out.

ELSIE. What shall I do now I haven't done any of that?

LIZ. Disco lights. There's some spotlights in a box over there.
Just put them up, will you? (*To* MIKE:) I don't know where I
am, now.

MIKE. Just relax, it's either going to be all right, or it's not.

LIZ. It's all very well saying Punch has had a colostomy, how am
I going to make a colostomy bag? How? When? It's eight
o'clock now.

MIKE. Don't bug me about time. (*Rips school-type clock off the
wall, and throws it through the window. Walks out.*)

LIZ. It was ten minutes slow anyway.

MIKE *comes in, goes to* LIZ *and kisses her.*

MIKE. I love you, OK.? Got a fiver?

LIZ. Course I have. Come back soon.

MIKE. Either I will, or I won't.

LIZ. Sure — I just wondered if you knew when.

MIKE *leaves.* LIZ *dials a number.*

(*Into the phone.*) Patsy? Liz. Can I have Lynne for tonight and all day tomorrow, please? . . . Catering, Cystitis Rally. Thanks . . . Perfectly under control, thank you. Bye.

ELSIE (*heaves nasty mess of cables out of the box, old spotlights, etc*). Frank?

FRANK (*in deep trouble with the booth*). I beg yours?

ELSIE. Sort that out will you?

FRANK. Certainly. Perhaps you can carry on with the er, kiosk. I've made a start. (*They swap places.*) Now, what do we want?

LIZ. Different colours, please, Frank. Spotlights flashing on and off, a disco-type thing. I'm worn out. Shall I make some tea?

ELSIE. Yeah, go on.

FRANK. Earth's blue, isn't it?

ELSIE. I don't think Gail's going to come now, do you?

LIZ. She still might. We never thought she'd send up those bras for the Ugandan Asians, but she did.

ELSIE. Yeh, pale green — 34D.

LIZ. What's 34D?

ELSIE. Well, that's like skinny little people with huge great bazonkas.

LIZ. So a 40A would be someone with a very wide back and a flat chest?

ELSIE. Yeh, men, they're called.

LIZ. What do you think of Mike?

ELSIE. Very nice.

LIZ. We live together.

ELSIE. Oh yes?

LIZ. He moved in a few weeks ago.

ELSIE. Really.

LIZ. And I moved out.

ELSIE. Why?

LIZ. There wasn't really room for me as well as Celia.

ELSIE. Celia?

LIZ. His wife.

ELSIE. Fine.

LIZ. Also, they thought it would be better for the kids if I wasn't there. I go back once a week to pay the rent, and clean up when Celia's at her Mum's, so that's OK. It's just, things aren't quite right with Mike.

ELSIE. Go on.

LIZ. Well, we're tremendously close in every way, but he doesn't seem to want to, sleep with me . . . you can't blame him with me, looking like this.

ELSIE. Cheer up, sex is nothing to write home about.

LIZ. Isn't it?

ELSIE. Would you? Dear Mum, am writing home about sex.

LIZ. It's all right for you, you did it when you were seventeen, you were the first.

ELSIE. I was the first in the scripture group. That's like being the first lemming to join the Samaritans.

LIZ. Do you fancy him?

ELSIE. No.

LIZ. Oh, why not?

ELSIE. Nothing personal. I've just gone off the whole thing.

LIZ. Have you?

ELSIE. Oh yes.

LIZ. You used to like it.

ELSIE. I know I did.

>   *Sings:*
>   **I've Had It Up To Here**
>
>   I've had it up to here with men —
>   Perhaps I should phrase that again.

Been spraying Woollies Number Nine on,
Knocking back the Microgynon,
Since I don't remember when.
I've had it up to here with blokes,
And all their stupid dirty jokes
About poofs and wogs and nigs and
Buying pokes in pigs and
Here's a funny one about John Noakes.

Men act as if to have a screw
Is the last thing that they want to do.
Then they switch the lights off,
And try and rip your tights off,
They take their coffee with sugar, milk and you.

To start your evening off in Lurex,
And finish it with Durex
Doesn't really turn me on.
I'll stay at home in my pyjamas,
Watch a programme about Llamas,
I won't need any lip-gloss,
I won't need any Amplex,
Just Ovaltine and buns for one.

It's not that I expect true love,
Or gazing at the Stars above --
If as a person, they'd acknowledge me,
Not bits of gynaecology,
Or if they'd just take off the rubber glove.

I've had it up to here with sex,
Those nylon vests and hairy necks.
They expect you to be flighty,
They act like God Almighty,
'Cos they've got a cock, and they can mend a flex.
When they proudly strip and pose,
I want to say 'What's one of those?'
They tend to feel a failure
If you don't love their genitalia,
Though why you should, Christ only knows.

No more nights of drinking,
Nodding, smiling, thinking
'Jesus, when can I go home?'
No more struggling in taxis,
In Vauxhalls, Imps and Maxis
With stupid little bleeders
With all the charming manners
Of the average garden gnome.

And when they're down to socks and grin,
You know it's time to get stuck in.
Full of self-congratulation,
They expect a combination
Of Olga Korbut, Raquel Welch
And Rin-Tin-Tin.
I've not had an encounter yet
That didn't leave me cold and wet.
I'd be happier, I know.
If we could only go
From the foreplay straight to the cigarette.

I'll finish and just say again,
I've definitely had it,
Well, very nearly had it,
Had it nearly up to here with men.

At the end of the song, ELSIE carries on with the booth, FRANK with the lights.

FRANK (*he plugs his light in, it works*)' Hoopla, as they say on the Bank Holiday Circus.

LIZ. Great, Frank. Do five or six more, and make them flash on and off, can you?

FRANK (*to* ELSIE). There doesn't seem to be a switch on it.

ELSIE. Can you plug it in and unplug it really fast?

The plug flares up. FRANK jumps back in panic, kicks it, hurts his foot, unplugs it.

ELSIE. Can you do that to music?

Doorbell rings. LIZ goes to answer it.

LIZ. If that's the woman collecting for the lepers . . .

ELSIE. Tell her we haven't got any.

LIZ (*pressing buzzer*). It's Lynne.

ELSIE. Who's Lynne?

LIZ. She works in the Salad Bar, but she's part of a Youth
Opportunities Scheme so one day a week she has compulsory
murals. They go out with tins of emulsion and cover old ladies'
houses with pictures of Elvis Costello. It's supposed to be the
history of modern music from ragtime to punk.

ELSIE. Any good?

LIZ. No, it's bloody awful, but the whole street is being
demolished in 1981 so it doesn't really matter. They tried to
put Louis Armstrong on the side of the Baptist Chapel but he
didn't show up.

FRANK. Is it true punks spit on people and jump up and down?

ELSIE. That's Dana you're thinking of.

LIZ. Come along Lynne, best foot forward.

LYNNE (*going over to* LIZ). Look, if it's about Paul McCartney's
left leg on the double doors at the back of the Corn Exchange,
I know it's right deformed, but I never said I could do legs.
I do grass mainly.

LIZ. No, that's fine — actually, I want you to put on your
catering hat this evening.

LYNNE. We don't wear hats. Mrs Harris has a beauty bonnet, but
that's only because she had a long-distance phone-call in the
middle of her home perm.

LIZ. No, it's just an expression.

LYNNE. What is?

LIZ. 'Putting on your catering hat.' Hat in this context meaning
role or job delineation.

LYNNE. Oh. I just wondered, 'cos of all them rumours about the
Salad Bar girls having to wear them PVC aprons with adverts
on the front.

LIZ. I hadn't heard about that. Is that going to happen?

LYNNE. Mrs Harris might be, but I've told them to stuff it. It's bad enough being up to your elbows in Quiche Lorraine, without walking around dressed as a bleeding sauce bottle.

LIZ. Now — introductions or instructions first?

LYNNE. Eh?

LIZ. Now, what I want you to do, you know we're having the cystitis party here tomorrow, so if you could just do the catering, all right? Now there's plenty of oats, and (*Looking in cupboards, getting sacks out.*) turmeric, and powder paint, you won't want that. Perhaps someone could paint the piano? Anyway, be as inventive as you like, and when you've got that on the go, perhaps you can do something imaginative with rice.

LYNNE. Boil it?

LIZ. Yes, lovely idea. You've made rice salad in the Salad Bar, haven't you?

LYNNE. You're not joking. I wouldn't mind, but it gets everywhere, I leave a bloody trail, me, when I finish work. Pigeons follow me home.

ELSIE, *who has been doing pretty well with the booth, stands up to stretch her legs.* FRANK, *who has climbed up somewhere with his spotlights, drops it onto the booth and just misses* ELSIE. *Pause.*

FRANK. I say, look out!

LIZ. Oh, and this is Elsie.

ELSIE. It nearly bloody wasn't.

LIZ. An old friend of mine; she's a waitress, too, so you should get on really well with each other. (*Pause — embarrassed silence.*) And Frank you probably recognise. He was part of the All-night Madrigal Event last week. Were you around for that?

LYNNE. No, but when we got in the next morning, the cat had been sick. We didn't know if it were the madrigals or that old Scotch egg it found behind the radiator.

LIZ. Where's Kev? I was hoping he could help out. We're just a tiny bit behind with the preparations. Kev's Lynne's boyfriend.

LYNNE. Fiancé.

LIZ. Really? Since when?

LYNNE. Since I passed my pregnancy test. I knew, though, before. I was sick every morning, sore boobs and my period's five weeks late, and I thinks to myself, it's not measles, is it?

LIZ. And what does Kev say?

LYNNE. He doesn't know. He'd run a mile if he knew I was up the duff. He's been asking me to marry him for yonks, but I've been telling him to get lost, 'cos (a) he's hardly Kevin Keegan, (b) he only wants to so he can leave home, get a flat and put his Scalextric all over the living-room floor, and (c) I know we're not compatible, 'cos I did a quiz. Still, what can you do?

ELSIE. Have an abortion.

LYNNE. I thought about it, but I can't stand being fiddled about with, do you know what I mean? I won't even wear rubber gloves to wash up.

ELSIE. It's the doctors that wear rubber gloves, not you.

LYNNE. I hate all that sort of thing, though. I was supposed to dissect a mouse once at school, but I couldn't. They had to give me a lupin. Can't stand guts. I can't really believe I've got all those things on the drawing in the Lil-let packet. I've put the oats in with the turmeric, is that all right?

LIZ (*not listening*). Yes, whatever you feel is best. You're the chef.

LYNNE (*chopping up garlic and throwing it in the pot*). I don't take much interest, really. I only like toast. I can't be doing with all this chucking cress everywhere, and bunging things up olives.

LIZ. If you only eat toast, it's probably lack of Vitamin E that makes you so aggressive.

LYNNE. Who says I'm aggressive?

LIZ (*moving away*). Anyway, I'm sure you know exactly what you're doing, and it's going to be delicious.

Enter MIKE.

LYNNE (*to herself*)' I don't and it isn't.

LIZ. Mike you know.

LYNNE. You owe us for two ploughman's and a beef curry. He said you'd pay. It's gone to my head, being pregnant -- I've been nice to Kev all day. I've not sworn at him, I've laughed at his jokes, I've let him eat pickled onions -- I'm going off my nut. (*Sits down near* MIKE, *lights a cigarette*.) And now I'm stuck with him for forty years.

MIKE. Hey, cool it.

LYNNE. I didn't even enjoy it. If it hadn't been *The Waltons* on, I'd never have bothered to do it in the first place.

MIKE. Calm down, it's all right.

LYNNE. It's all right for men. You just take it out wipe it and put it back. My Dad'll go mad. He's deranged enough now -- he has been ever since he banged his head on the cistern, celebrating the World Cup.

ELSIE. But you want to get married, don't you? It won't be that bad if you have to leave home.

LYNNE. I don't want to get married. I'd leave the whole sodding mess behind if I could but where could I go? I've had it.

MIKE (*puts his arm around her* -- LIZ *notices*, FRANK *is fiddling around with something, and* ELSIE *is listening*). You don't have to do anything you don't want. I'm setting up a place in Wales.

LIZ. That's a lovely idea, Mike.

LYNNE. What is?

LIZ. You'd really like it, Lynne, it's a community, it's going to be in tepees, they'll be arranged in a special pattern, according to the position of Uranus.

MIKE. The Dog Star.

LYNNE. What's it for?

LIZ. Well, everyone'll chop wood together, and weave wool from the hedgerows, and celebrate . . .

LYNNE. Celebrate what?

LIZ. The winter solstice, and so on.

MIKE. It'll be really good, Lynne, just you and the baby and a lot of friends, and no hassles. Sounds good, yeah?

LYNNE. Are you going to it?

LIZ. Yes, later on . . .

MIKE. Liz can't, I'm afraid. It's only for people with kids.

LIZ. Is it?

MIKE. You going to come, Lynne? I'd really like you to.

LIZ. Lynne would hate it, Mike, stuck in the middle of a field, no telly, no Osmonds.

LYNNE. I hate the bloody Osmonds.

MIKE (leaving). Just remember I care about you and keep cool. See you tomorrow.

LYNNE. He's quite nice, him, isn't he? (Carries on cooking.) How can I have a baby? I've never even had a goldfish. I don't know where Kev's got to. Just my luck if he falls for another bird tonight.

ELSIE. Why would he?

LYNNE. He's mental, that's why. You've only got to see where he's tattooed to know that.

FRANK. I say, I wouldn't mind doing the old disc jockey bit tomorrow, reading the labels and so on.

ELSIE. Hey, Liz, how do you fancy Frank doing the disco tomorrow?

LIZ. What? Yeah, fine. I'm not really bothered, actually. I'm thinking of ringing Biddy up, and packing the job in.

ELSIE. Why?

LIZ. Well, it seems a bit pointless paying the mortgage on something, when I can't even live there, because I haven't got a baby, and I'm never likely to get one, am I, when Mike won't come near me, and if Lynne's swanning off to North Wales with Kev's brat, well, she can bloody well pay for their donkeys and their chemical toilets herself.

LYNNE. I'm not going to North Wales. I won't be going anywhere for sixteen years, will I, stuck at home smelling of milk, watching the horse racing, staring at a tiny lump of Kev gobbing egg all over its face. I'll thump it, I know I will.

LIZ. I'd really like to have a baby.

LYNNE. Have bleeding mine then.

Pause.

LIZ. Yes, I will, if you don't mind, thanks. I'll take it off you when it's born, OK? When's it due?

LYNNE. I dunno. I don't keep track of my periods much, I like surprises.

FRANK (*backing away*). Terminal screwdriver.

LYNNE. Will you really take it off me? Bring it up, and all that?

LIZ. Certainly. It'll be good for me, the responsibility. They sleep for the first six months anyway, don't they? Mike's going to be thrilled when I tell him.

LYNNE. Kev won't know what's bloody hit him, when he comes in. Just think, I even offered to play with his Scalextric. He can stuff that. Hey, great, cheers, fag anybody?

Sings:

Turned Out Nice Again

Never been a one to have a carry-on
When I felt merry.
Don't wear funny hats or get a bit far-gone
On Champagne perry.
And I've never blown those squeaky things
The ones with feathers on the end.
Trying to show I'm happy drives me round the bend.

Never liked those meals that you're supposed to eat
For celebrating.
Irish coffee, tiny chips and lumps of meat,
And being kept waiting.
Now what could beat a
Bit of cheese on a Ryvita
In front of the TV.
When it comes to celebrating, there's something
    wrong with me.

I'd really like to show you that I'm glad I've come,
If you understand me.
I could stick a label, 'happy' on my bum,
Where would it land me?
I'd love to be the kind of person
That could absolutely go berserk,
But somehow for me I don't think it would work.

If I try a military two step or a waltz,
Then I just get harassed.
I've got no sense of rhythm,
So I just become embarrassed.
I can't run along a
Street and do the conga,
I only wish I could,
You'll just have to take my word that I feel good.

Unless you are an idiot, you've got the gist,
I'm not complaining.
Cartwheels are right out, I've got a funny wrist —
Well, when it's raining.
But when you've been depressed
And someone solves your problems,
That's the moment when
You want to quote George Formby, say 'It's turned
    out nice again'.

Nasty silence.

LIZ. You can play the piano.

ELSIE. I know that.

LIZ. You can play it for the party.

ELSIE. I only know one thing.

LIZ. Play it.

> ELSIE *plays it.*

> What's that?

ELSIE. Jamaican Rumba.

LIZ. Do it again.

> *She does.*

> I thought it went . . . (*Sings it.*)

ELSIE. It does. That's the top half of the duet — I only know the bottom half.

LIZ. Anyway, that's Punch and Judy, duets, and how about you, Lynne?

LYNNE. What?

LIZ. Well, you're w king class, what about doing a turn for us — Gracie Fields impression, or a monologue in dialect, or clog-dancing — I expect you're good at that, aren't you?

LYNNE. What is it?

> LIZ *demonstrates a few steps.*

> If you're so full of it, you do it. I've never heard of it — is it Dutch?

> *Enter KEV, a bit pissed.*

LYNNE. How did you get in, wasn't the front door shut?

KEV. Kicked it down, Bionic man me.

LYNNE. Shut up, you.

> KEV *lumbers over to* LYNNE, *who pushes him away.*

> Stop breathing on me, dummy, you get on my bloody nerves, you do.

KEV. What's up with you — you were all over me at quarter past seven.

LYNNE. There's no need to be so bloody accurate about it.

KEV. It was so unusual, I looked at my watch. Like you would if you'd seen a murder.

LYNNE. Oh, shut up.

KEV. You said I made you go all funny inside.

LYNNE. Well, I've changed my mind.

KEV. Oh, well. What are you doing, anyway?

LIZ. We're getting ready for the party.

KEV. There's no balloons.

ELSIE. Balloons!

LIZ. Yes — I've got some. Two hundred, in fact. (*Going to drawer.*) I was supposed to send them somewhere for Christmas, it's a good job I didn't, isn't it? Now, Lynne, can you leave the cooking for a minute?

LYNNE. I can leave it all night, I don't think it's going to get any better now.

LIZ. If you'd just like to make a start on these balloons, just do a hundred or so for now, Frank can tie the knots in them. Oh, look! (*Holds up a lot of packets of paper strips for Christmas paper chains.*) Now, this is a nice job, Elsie.

ELSIE. Yes, you'll enjoy yourself there.

LIZ. Well, actually, I was going to get on with the booth, unless you'd rather.

ELSIE (*taking chains*). No, go on. Why don't you get Kev to do the booth, and then you could have a lie down.

LIZ. No, I can't really have a lie down just yet, though God knows I need it, but Kev — do you see this, would you like to give us a hand, and fit it together?

KEV. I don't mind. There's nothing else doing tonight.

LYNNE. Shut up, you.

KEV *puts the booth together,* FRANK *and* ELSIE *start on the paper chains,* LYNNE *blows up a balloon, and makes it squeak.*

LIZ. Lynne.

LYNNE. What?

LIZ. Please. (LYNNE *stops, crushed*.) Thank you.

ELSIE. Bloody hell, you never lose that old Head Girl's authority do you?

LYNNE. Was she Head Girl?

ELSIE. She was everything. Head Girl, House Captain, Librarian. She had so many badges she had to be pushed round in a wheelbarrow.

LIZ. It's true — not about the wheelbarrow, but I practically ran that school single-handed. I did everything.

ELSIE. She did. Came in at seven to stoke the boilers.

LIZ. And I won loads of prizes.

ELSIE. Not more than Gail.

LIZ. What did she get that I didn't?

ELSIE. She won that prize for socially responsible behaviour.

LIZ. What was it?

ELSIE. A hand grenade. And she beat you into second place for the Good Manners shield.

LYNNE. Who did?

LIZ. Gail — she was in our form. I'll get my own back on her one day.

ELSIE. Not tonight though, pity.

LYNNE. What is?

ELSIE. Well, we thought it would be a laugh if we could get her here for an Old Girls' Reunion tonight. So we sent her this fake letter. Didn't we?

LIZ. It's ages ago, what did we say?

ELSIE. I can't remember. Hang on; 'Dear Old Girl'.

LYNNE. Dear Old Girl?

ELSIE. Dear *Old* Girl, Friday the whatever, is the 25th anniversary bla bla. School song 8.30; tombola 8.35. What else?

LIZ. Something about coming in your gym knickers.

ELSIE. No. I know, please arrive in games uniform.

LIZ. Please arrive in games uniform, hockey boots.

LIZ. } And needlework apron.
ELSIE. }

LIZ. Fancy dress. Funny hats?

ELSIE. Novelty headgear, prizes will be given for novelty headgear taking the theme of 'That Old Black Magic'. You thought of that, that was brilliant.

LYNNE. She hasn't come though has she?

Doorbell rings.

FRANK. It's Betty from Candy Cosmetics.

LIZ. Let him in. Betty's only a superb drag artist, isn't he, he's crazy about me and owes me a favour. That's the cabaret sorted out. Candy Cosmetics must be his new character.

LYNNE. I hope this one's better than his Farrah Fawcett-Majors. Nothing like her in a bikini.

FRANK. Why not?

LYNNE. Well, he had right hairy legs, for one thing.

FRANK. Wondered what you were going to say then.

LYNNE. You mean you hoped I was going to say his dick stuck out — well, it didn't, it was very realistic, satisfied?

FRANK (*backing off*). I think I've dropped my styptic pencil, back in a min. (*He heads towards the loo. There is a knock on the door.*)

LIZ. Come in.

BETTY (*off*). I'm sorry, I never lay my hand on a strange knob.

LIZ (*opens the door*). That's amazing.

BETTY. It's just a regulation, but it oils the wheels of commerce. Good evening everybody.

LYNNE.⎫ Evening.
ELSIE. ⎭

LIZ. I can't get over it — come in -- you're an answer to a prayer.

BETTY (*still in doorway*). Now don't tell me you've had sleepless nights over your open pores, you're as bad as my daughter-in-law. (*Takes out a small jar, hands it to* LIZ.) Smooth that over your greasy centre panel tonight, sleep on your back, you'll have skin like a tambourine in the morning.

LIZ. Sit down.

BETTY. No, I'm not moving an inch until you've scanned my credentials. There's far too many people roaming the streets, deceiving senior citizens with a trench coat and a rubber torch. (*Hands* LIZ *an identification card.*)

ELSIE. He's very good, isn't he?

LYNNE. It isn't him.

LIZ. Thank you. That's fine.

BETTY (*coming in*). I know what you're thinking, you're right, that photo was taken before I had my streaks done, it makes a tremendous difference, doesn't it? It lifts the face. It does. It lifts it. As you can see, my full name's Anne Hyphen Elizabeth, but they said at the office, Betty, we can't get it on the one badge, and they were quite right, they couldn't.

LIZ. I thought you were someone else.

BETTY. Well, I ask you, do I look like someone else? Now, first things first. Let me make it crystal clear that you are not obliged to purchase.

LIZ (*getting ready to see her off*). That's fine. Thank you very much.

BETTY (*settling in*). Though, obviously, one isn't trudging from door to door with a hereditary hip complaint for nothing. Now, may I use your table? Don't say no — use up too many of that little word, and you could find yourself with nothing to say in a sticky situation. (*Opens up a huge pink suitcase — displays huge racks of rows of bright pink cosmetics.*) Shall we start with you, dear? Are those tints natural?

LYNNE *looks down at her chest.*

We'll give you the benefit of the doubt, though what they can do with henna these days is nobody's business. (*She dabs perfume on* LYNNE's *wrist.*) We recommend this for a redhead. It's mainly musk, and let's face it, you never see a frigid polecat. And last? I should say so. I spilt some on my husband's gardening trousers the previous October, and he was still getting funny looks from the dustmen when they came round for their Christmas box. That smell will stay with you, don't you worry. Only £3.90 for the splash-on, and when it's empty, it converts into a salt-pot. Now, I'm going to be a bit controversial now, I'll probably set you three girls at each others' throats -- I'm going to tell you Powder Blusher is on the way out! You're stunned, aren't you? I was taken aback myself, when Mr McBurnie broke it to me. But these new pencils are marvellous because you can put it where you want it, which is half the battle. (*Dabs at* LIZ's *face.*) Now blend that lightly yourself. I'm not one of these make-up ladies forever taking a poke at your cheekbones.

Dabbing at the girls' faces, bringing out eye shadow to put on their wrists while she speaks. In a complete flurry of compacts, lipsticks, etc., trying them on the girls, on herself, putting them back, etc.

(*To* LIZ:) Now, I don't know if you're troubled by sebum at all, but it will block your pores given half a chance, and I don't think you've been as thorough with a slice of cucumber as you might be, have you? I may sell commercial products, but I have to be fair. I have seen wonders done with Fuller's Earth and a couple of old teabags. So what I'm saying — what's your name, dear?

LIZ. Liz.

BETTY. What I'm saying, Liz, is this: if you do get a little black visitor, don't squeeze it — unless your hands are covered in a sterilised silk hanky, which, let's face it, chances they won't be. Don't squeeze — cover it up with our push-up blemish concealer; three shades, fair, beige, and tawny for those of us with the compulsory sun-tans, and don't they make good nurses? Now, we've a nice line in Zodiac powder compacts. What sign are you, dear?

ELSIE. Taurus.

BETTY. Now, we haven't a Taurus, but the Gemini's a pretty colour, don't you think. My son's on the cusp but you'd never know to look at him. (*To* LYNNE:) Now, you're young enough to love a gimmick. (*Taking out some kind of stuffed toy with cosmetics inside it.*) Now, isn't he cute? And all the shades are matched — such a boon for the fashion-conscious colour-blind. These were Mr Thornton's idea originally, he really is a brilliant person, and kind! He conducts a choir of over two hundred agoraphobics, mainly sopranos for some reason. Such a shame, because they can never have an annual outing.

By now she is packing up a few things for each girl, taking it for granted they will buy them.

There's so many of them, it's a wonder they can all see his baton. Mr. Thornton says he really needs one six-foot long with a red light on the end. So that's £1.28 for the blemish concealer, the compact is £3, now don't flinch, it's refillable, and Betty Bear, they claim they didn't call her after me, but I have my doubts, just £6.50.

The girls pay. Enter FRANK.

(*Shuts case and relaxes.*) So, what goes on here? It looks very . . . happy-go-lucky.

LIZ. Well, basically, it's an adaptable space.

BETTY. Like a church hall?

LIZ. Well, we like to think it's more of a place where people can let themselves go.

BETTY. Like a Scout hut. So, what am I interrupting? A little production? A spot of drama?

LIZ. We're just preparing for a party tomorrow. Look it's a service we provide for large organisations.

BETTY. And which organisation is it tomorrow?

LIZ. The cystitis sufferers.

BETTY. Oh, lovely. So, tell me about the party — what have you got lined up?

LIZ. Well, Lynne here is doing the catering, she's got a very nice line in . . . what do you call it, Lynne?

LYNNE. Oats.

BETTY. Oat cuisine. Carry on, Liz.

LIZ. And Elsie's going to play the piano.

BETTY. Lovely, what are you going to play?

ELSIE. The bottom half of Jamaican Rumba.

BETTY. Well, it's the bottom that matters in a rumba, isn't it?

LIZ. And Frank is doing the disco.

BETTY. And have you got one of those lovely portable disco things you can get nowadays?

FRANK. No, but we'll probably get a gramophone from somewhere. Plenty of time, isn't there, Liz?

LIZ. Oh, yes, anything can happen in this business.

BETTY. But isn't this party tomorrow?

LIZ. Yes.

BETTY. And that's all you've got?

LIZ. And part of a pig.

BETTY. It's hardly a running buffet and the Three Degrees, is it? You know what I think you need?

LIZ. What?

BETTY. To be blunt — me. Don't be fooled by these laughter lines — 'Thoroughly Modern Betty' they used to call me at out-patients. If I ever have a gravestone — you see I have been thinking of having my ashes scattered over the Peak District — I should like that lovely word 'Modern' in letters three foot high. It sums me up — it does — it sums me up. Do you know what I'm going to do for you? I'm only going to reveal my disco-dancing aren't I? I did Spanish Hustle for the diabetics last month -- it brought tears to their eyes -- it did. And you'll adore Daddy -- he can do his novelty hedge-trimming as seen at the Co-Op. Of course there's Daddy's joke -- the funniest story in the world providing he can remember the punchline. I'm only forgetting my son aren't I? Lucky for you I was feeling generous on the night of August Bank Holiday 1947. I don't like to boast, but he's a little smasher. He's like me but with a set of doings. His Shirley Abicair impression has to be seen to be believed. Now where did I stuff the zither. Even the woman next door has admitted he's charismatic, and she's disliked us since November 5th 1967 when the Catherine Wheel flew off the horse chestnut and singed her pussy. See you tomorrow. Toodle-oo.

Exit BETTY.

LIZ. Great. That's what Community Arts is all about. Now, let's get this place cleaned up -- Frank, that's your job. Lynne, you're in charge of murals.

KEV (*having put booth up*). I've done it.

LIZ. Great. There's three hundred cups in the toilet, rinse them out, can you?

Gives ELSIE *a ball of string.*

When you've finished blowing up the balloons, can you improvise a kind of net with this, so we can let them all down at the end? OK.? Well, I think the hard work's paid off. I can't think anything untoward will happen now.

Enter GAIL, *dressed in games uniform, needlework apron, hockey boots, holding a blue and green banana, and wearing on her head a huge dice, with playing cards protruding from it on wires.*

GAIL. Hi. The door was open. Where's your novelty headgear.

ALL. Look out!

The booth collapses.

ACT TWO

Saturday midday. The whole place has been cleaned up, the walls painted very badly, balloons are suspended in a net, paper chains are up, stew on the stove, wine and cups laid out on tables.

LIZ is asleep on the floor. ELSIE is wandering about half-dressed, making tea. GAIL is fully dressed.

GAIL. Oh, and do you remember Christine Palmer, she's got two kiddies now, one of them's backward, or something. Valerie Barton, not seen her since she got engaged to a Spaniard, shouldn't think that's worked out. Mavis Lumb is Head of Department, too, Domestic Sci, smaller school than mine though, not such an achievement. Do you remember Heapy?

ELSIE. Yes.

GAIL. She had to come out of college when she fell expecting, she had an IUD but it slipped due to her trampolining. She demonstrates magnetic window cleaners now. £4.99, I believe they are.

ELSIE. They don't even work, those. Either they cover the whole window in dirty foam, or they fall off and kill people in the street.

GAIL. Mmm, that's what she said. Did you hear about Hilary?

ELSIE. No. Is she dead?

GAIL. Married an Indian social worker. The colour of a cup of cocoa, I heard.

   ELSIE *takes tea over to* LIZ.

ELSIE. Oi, it's twelve o'clock.

LIZ. Thanks. How long have I been asleep?

ELSIE. Twelve hours.

LIZ. Really? What time did you get to bed?

ELSIE. Half eight.

LIZ. You must be quite tired, then. What did you sleep on?

ELSIE. Gail had the coconut mats, and I had the blackout curtains.

LIZ. Was it OK.?

ELSIE. Yes, except I had terrible dreams about Neville Chamberlain.

LIZ. Hi, Gail.

GAIL. Good morning.

LIZ. You're going to stay for the party, aren't you?

GAIL. I've promised Frank I'll help him make the sandwiches. He's just gone out for bread. I'm going to show him my special butter spreading method. (*Pause.*) You scrape it on and scrape it off. Just something I learned at college.

LIZ (*slowly getting up and wandering about*). Oh, you made the net. I told you it was easy. Anybody rung up?

ELSIE. Someone rang and said they hadn't been paid yet — some theatre group — Launderdrama.

LIZ. Oh, them. They do shows in launderettes.

ELSIE. That must be really irritating. It's bad enough being in the launderette in the first place, without three idiots in stripy socks bursting in and making jokes about the Common Market.

LIZ. You don't know what you're talking about.

ELSIE. I do. A theatre group did a show about housewives outside Tesco's in the Arndale Centre last summer, and they all had stripy socks on, and made jokes about Margaret Thatcher. And they're standing in Tesco's doorway shouting out 'Housewives of Britain, what do you want?' And they're all going 'We want to get into Tesco's!'

GAIL. I think the High-Street price war has been very beneficial.

ELSIE. What?

GAIL. Elsie tells me you're going camping. I can recommend the hostel near the Hawkshead Ferry, if you get rained out.

LIZ. No, I'm joining a kind of commune, with my bloke, Mike, and our baby. Well, it's Lynne's foetus, but we're having it as soon as it's born. I can't wait to tell Mike.

GAIL. And what will you do in this commune?

LIZ. Well, we'll be living in a field on what we can pick up.

ELSIE. Sheep droppings, old johnnies, nice.

LIZ. Now, come on, let's be nice to each other. What have we got in common?

ELSIE. Ovaries.

LIZ. For one thing — you both play the piano.

GAIL. We had the same teacher.

ELSIE. The Jamaican Rumba freak.

GAIL. I learnt that one, rather a chirpy tune, I thought.

LIZ. You can play it together, then, for the party, can't you? We'll open the show with it.

GAIL. Well, I don't know. I'm not so limber as I was.

ELSIE. I'll give it a go. Just let me finish my tea.

LIZ. I hope the physical side of our relationship develops before we move to Wales.

ELSIE. Our relationship?

LIZ. Me and Mike. I don't want to be the only one in the tepee not making embarrassing noises.

GAIL. You see, I have a Bontempi electric organ now, so I haven't played chords for ages.

ELSIE. If you want to sleep with him, tell him.

LIZ. I was sort of hoping it might happen by accident.

ELSIE. Not very likely, unless you get trapped overnight in a mixed sauna with nothing to read.

GAIL. The chords are automatic. You press a button.

ELSIE. Rightio. Shall we have a go, then?

GAIL. Well, I'd like to practise it first.

ELSIE. You'd like to practise it before we practise it?

GAIL. I suppose you hope you're joking. (*Sits at the piano.*)

LIZ. If I did tell him, and we did go to bed together, I wouldn't want to put him off by inadequacy of technique.

ELSIE. It's not like a driving test. I am so sorry to have to inform you that your intercourse does not reach the required standard. Are you ready?

LIZ. Well, you know, I only did it that once.

ELSIE. With your erudite oriental.

LIZ. It's not everyone that's done it with a Chinese librarian.

ELSIE. True, I still maintain it would have been easier to pay the fine. Now listen — the famous piece for four hands, three of them mine, Jamaican Rumba. One, two, one two three four . . .

They play, both of them playing the same part, therefore there is no tune. They stop eventually.

What happened to — (*Whistles the tune.*) I do the rumba, you do the Jamaican.

GAIL. I didn't learn the treble part, Mrs Beaver always took that.

ELSIE. She did with me as well. What a bloody awful piano teacher, turning out hundreds of people who can't play anything above the keyhole.

GAIL. I think it was because the bass-player traditionally manipulates the pedals, and she was unable to do that because of her knee.

ELSIE. Don't remind me. I'll never forget the smell of hot surgical stocking and 4711.

GAIL. I didn't do Mozart. (ELSIE *falls to the floor.*) I changed to Domestic Science in Lower V.

ELSIE. Look, do you want to go and buy the sheet-music? Make it a bit more worthwhile you're being here.

GAIL. You're not working up to an apology, by any chance?

ELSIE. No.

GAIL. I spent £8.76 on a weekend return to come here, £3 on taxis, and that's without tipping, because I never do, because I think it's a pernicious practice. I had a new sponge-bag to come away with, and that damned banana wasn't cheap, either.

ELSIE. What about your novelty headgear taking the theme of 'That Old Black Magic', splash out on that, did you?

GAIL. I had that by me. Well, I'm waiting.

ELSIE. What?

GAIL. I'm waiting for an apology.

ELSIE. But I'm not sorry.

GAIL. I don't see what that's got to do with it.

ELSIE. We did it for a joke. It gave us a laugh. Just because those words don't come in a bleeding recipe book doesn't mean they don't exist. It must be awful being you — mingeing about all day, poking at people's Cornish pasties, going home to a pile of exercise books. 'Stuffed Eggs — how they can enhance the tea-table.' What do you do in the holidays? Wash yourself, iron yourself and put yourself away?

GAIL. I go to a cousin on the Isle of Mull. It's very restful.

ELSIE. I bet it is. One day, you'll wake up and say 'Oh, look, my heart's stopped beating.'

GAIL. What are you implying?

ELSIE. I am implying that you exhibit all the joie de vivre of a half-eaten meat-and-potato pie.

Sings:

Make A Joke

Ever heard of being happy?
Ever heard of fun?
Why this wonderful impression
Of a hot-cross bun?

Why are you so miserable?
Life is not about
Sucking a bronchitis pastille
As the fire goes out.

Am I making any contact?
Am I making sense?
Are you taking evening classes
In being bleeding dense?
Other people somewhere, somehow
Do not just exist —
They play nude Monopoly
They go out and they get well pissed.

I am begging, pleading with you
On my bended brains —
This world is one enormous bottom,
You're one of the pains.
This will not be held against you,
Will not go on file,
I promise this will go no further
If you just go mad — and smile!

You've got the necessary muscles
Nothing vital is going to fall
Off.
I know that probably you'd get
Much more enjoyment from a nasty
Cough.
I'm pleading with you, baby,
Don't you think that maybe
You could smile?

How can one sane healthy person
Be so devoid of joy?
Cast away with you or Roy Plomley,
I'd have to go for Roy.
God forbid the comic's nightmare
Ever should come true-
Playing first house Glasgow Empire
And the only person there is you.

If it was up to you, comedians would not be paid in
Money.
Jokes would be illegal, you'd have to have a
    licence to be
Funny.
On behalf of old Dan Leno,
Max Miller and The Beano —
Up you.

I don't know your sense of humour,
What makes you shriek with mirth.
It could be an ugly rumour,
Could be Harry Worth,
Could be Brian Rix's trousers,
Or watching someone choke —
Do you think just once this weekend,
You could make a bleeding joke?

Doesn't have to be nothing sophisticated,
Like the one about the marrow and the nun,
Something out of Bunty,
Just so we know you have a sense of fun.

I'm getting too excited,
I'm going up in smoke.
Please, please, please, please
Just make a joke.

GAIL. I'll go and get the music for the duet then. Do you know
who wrote it?

ELSIE. I don't think anyone's owned up yet.

LIZ. I suppose I ought to get up and do something in a minute.
(*Pause*.) You know Mike?

ELSIE. No.

LIZ. Perhaps you're right and I should confront him with my libido.

ELSIE. Well, you'd better get it out of its cage because he'll be
here in a minute.

LIZ. What?

ELSIE. I rang him up. I told him to come over, you haven't sorted out the Punch and Judy yet.

LIZ (*leaping around*). Where are my bloody clothes? Have you got a comb?

ELSIE. Calm down – it's only Mike, it's not the Virgin Mary on a unicycle.

LIZ. I don't expect you to understand. We have a really special thing going.

ELSIE. You don't live with him, you don't sleep with him, you just hand over money. I have exactly the same relationship with the Inland Revenue.

A pig's body is thrown through the door.

LYNNE. I'm just going back to Lost Property. Kev thinks he's left its head on the bus.

ELSIE. Do we eat this or climb the North face and claim it for Britain.

LIZ. If I stand it in the sun do you think it'll defrost by six o'clock?

ELSIE. No. Turkeys take ages and even then they can kill you.

LIZ. I just think if I could develop my relationship with Mike I could achieve total mental and physical satisfaction.

ELSIE. I don't know why you don't just settle for a vibrator, a library book and a bar of chocolate.

LIZ. Perhaps I could relax about the sexual side if I could do it with someone else first.

ELSIE. What, practise on someone?

LIZ. Yes.

ELSIE. Who?

FRANK *pokes his head round the door.*

FRANK. Anything I can do?

ELSIE. I wouldn't, Liz.

FRANK. I've got two round ones and an awfully long one.

ELSIE. Oh well, in that case.

FRANK. I have a contribution from my mother towards the
refreshments. Half a pound of Liquorice Allsorts. Where's
Gail?

LIZ. She's gone to get some music.

FRANK. Well I'll commence slicing but I don't really want to
spread under my own steam.

ELSIE. Look — you mess it up with blokes because you try too
hard. If you'd have fancied Benjamin Franklyn he'd have
been in bed while you poked about with a kite and a coat
hanger inventing electricity. Don't be so keen. You jump into
these relationships like some all-year-round swimmer breaking
the ice on the Serpentine.

LIZ. Lay off a bit, you mean. Be more aloof.

ELSIE. Well . . .

Enter BETTY *and* MAURICE *on the march.*

BETTY.   ⎫   Further complications then ensued not helped
MAURICE. ⎬   by the fact that Divvi, the Co-op Cat, was
        ⎭   trapped in the Snack Bar.

BETTY. Morning girls. Maurice is in a tangle with his joke. Keep
moving Daddy, the girls aren't dressed.

BETTY.   ⎫   Now Divvi was a most peculiar cat with one
MAURICE. ⎬   very interesting habit. (*They march into the*
        ⎭   *toilet.*) Many's the time . . .

ELSIE. Hey I tell you what — if Mike thought you fancied Frank
he might get jealous and clasp you to his manly bosom.

LIZ. Sounds like *Woman's Realm.*

ELSIE. It was. I read it at the dentist's.

LIZ. What happened?

ELSIE. Two fillings and a scale and polish.

Enter MIKE, *smiling.*

MIKE. Hi.

ELSIE. Hello.

LIZ. Whisky? (*Remembering to be aloof.*) There isn't any.

MIKE. That's OK.

LIZ (*shouting*). Carry on Frank, it was fascinating.

FRANK. Beg pardon. Sorry. What?

LIZ. There's no need to stop talking just because Mike's here. It's not as if he was more important than anyone else.

MIKE. That's very true — each soul has infinite potential.

LIZ. Come and sit here Frank. Is there anything you'd specially like to say to me?

FRANK. A friend of my mother's will only swat wasps with a rolled-up copy of the Daily Mail. He says the ink contains an anaesthetic.

LIZ. Carry on.

FRANK. That's all there is to that one really.

LIZ. Frank and I have been discussing the possibility of going away together, Mike.

MIKE. Great.

LIZ. In his caravan. It's very small and intimate.

MIKE. Smashing.

FRANK. Actually it's got a lounge/dinette and a rockery.

LIZ. You see I think a woman should be free to pursue her sexual gratification in whatever direction she chooses.

MIKE. Absolutely.

FRANK. It's really more of a mobile home.

MIKE. Anyone fancy a drink? Liz — you got any money?

LIZ. No.

MIKE. I have, I'll treat you.

LIZ. No it's all right, you don't want me — you go with Elsie.

MIKE. All right. (*To* ELSIE:) You coming?

ELSIE. Yes. (*Exits.*)

LIZ. There is some whisky left, I just remembered.

MIKE. It's OK. — you have it. (*Exits.*)

FRANK. I don't carry them on me, but I could slip home. They're concealed under my winter underpants.

LIZ. Just go away.

BETTY. Do you think I could possibly come out of the toilet Liz? It's getting rather oppressive even for a happily married couple.

LIZ. Yes, sorry.

BETTY *comes out, hears droning from* MAURICE *as door opens.*

BETTY. Frank, just the person. Can you help me display my chutney. It's all in that box there.

LIZ. Betty —

BETTY. Pet?

LIZ. If you were keen on somebody and they only liked you as a friend, what would you do?

BETTY. Well it may not be your style, lamb, but I'd dress up like the proverbial canine's lunch.

MAURICE (*coming out*). Betty — what happens after 'Blow me down if his paws weren't stuck in the trifle'?

BETTY. Darling, this is Liz. Liz, this is my husband, Maurice. Liz is one of my lame ducks.

LIZ. Hello.

BETTY. Now, what would you like him to do first?

LIZ. Well, I haven't got round to fixing up the lighting yet.

MAURICE. Lights, eh? What do you want? Spots? Fresnels? Where's the control room?

LIZ. It's more of a cardboard box, really. (*Indicates hideous mess of cables, etc.*)

MAURICE (*sharp intake of breath acting*). Got twenty years, have you?

LIZ *laughs ingratiatingly.*

You want me to sort this lot out?

LIZ. If you could.

MAURICE. Someone wants shooting. It's like Heinz Spaghetti in here, it's like Heinz Spaghetti.

LIZ. Well, if you could just fix up a couple of spotlights to light the stage, that shouldn't be too difficult, should it?

MAURICE. You don't know what you're asking, my dear. I'll have a go, but I haven't seen connections like this since the Church Hall caught fire.

BETTY. Ooh, careful, darling, this is a Church Hall.

LIZ. Actually, it's an adaptable space.

BETTY *begins to put up the bunting, nipping from side to side of the room.*

BETTY. Pet — hadn't you better plug in the Hitachi? I must have a little practice, and anyway, I'm sure Liz will want to hear 'Boogie Bus' — it'll really put us in the mood.

MAURICE *gets out the stereo, and sets it up. Enter* FRANK.

LIZ *heads towards the bathroom.*

You're dipping your visage into hot H20, are you, Liz?

LIZ. Yes.

BETTY. Dig well in round the nostrils. It pays dividends.

LIZ *goes to the bathroom with 20 Benson and Hedges and a magazine.*

MAURICE *puts a record on the stereo.* BETTY *combines nipping about with a few disco dance steps.*

I wish I could remember that hitch-hike thing Mrs Fiske showed us last week, it would finish the whole thing off marvellously.

MAURICE. That leg thing, you mean?

BETTY. No, I got that off weeks ago. (*To* FRANK:) Men! (FRANK *joins in, then remembering he's supposed to be one.*)

No. It's a roly-poly one and a roly-poly two and you throw your arms up, oh, sorry, Frank — but there's a kind of bump to it, perhaps it'll come to me.

Enter LYNNE *and* KEV *with a pig's head.*

BETTY. Morning you two. Having a stab at brawn?

LYNNE. It's for the party. Kev left it on the bus. They wouldn't give it us back at first, the bloody man wanted us to describe it.

BETTY. Kev, dear, the booth suffered overnight, do you mind?

KEV. Oh, bloody hell, all right.

MAURICE *is doing, or rather not doing the lights.* KEV *builds the booth.* BETTY *is on bunting,* FRANK *unpacking* BETTY's *stuff,* LYNNE *unwraps the pig's head.*

LYNNE. Well, what shall I do with this?

BETTY. Well as I say, you could have a go at brawn, but it's rather a lengthy process.

FRANK. Don't you have to weight it down?

BETTY. I think you do, Frank, yes.

FRANK. My mother uses an old flat-iron.

BETTY. Does she? Has she not got an electric one?

FRANK. Oh yes, but she doesn't do the brawn with it.

BETTY. Oh, I see.

LYNNE. I'm not doing the brawn, am I, whatever bleeding brawn is — will someone tell me what to do with this pig's head, it's turning me over.

BETTY. Well, slice it, dear, and put it on a doily.

LYNNE. I've just got it from the freezer centre, it's rock hard.

BETTY. In that case, dust it and put an apple in its mouth.

LYNNE. What for?

BETTY. Atmosphere.

LYNNE *unwraps it, and writes 'atmosphere' on a piece of paper, and sticks it in front of the pig's head.*

Enter GAIL.

GAIL. Those stairs.

BETTY. It's Robb Wilton. Good afternoon — willing helper, or bladder sufferer?

GAIL. I'm the victim of a practical joke.

BETTY. Oh, lovely. Do you remember, Maurice, when the Boy sewed up the bottoms of your pyjama trousers? I couldn't stop laughing.

MAURICE. I could.

FRANK. Did you get your music, Gail?

GAIL. Nobody's heard of it. If it isn't Ian Dury, they haven't got it.

BETTY. Same with food. If it's not in a box with writing on it, they don't want to know, the young. I shouldn't think my son's so much as set eyes on a piece of raw liver since his honeymoon. What's that notice for, Lynne?

LYNNE. I'm putting 'atmosphere' on it, so people know not to eat it. It's like iron.

FRANK. Shall we, er, spread, Gail?

GAIL. Why not?

FRANK. You could carry on telling me that awfully funny story about the netball teacher's trouser suit.

GAIL. Oh yes, it was hilarious. I nearly laughed.

LYNNE. I feel sick.

FRANK. Oh, gosh, do you want me to do anything?

LYNNE. Yeah, piss off.

FRANK *is at a loss.*

GAIL. Take no notice, it's just adolescent bravado, I see it all the time.

FRANK. Thanks, Gail.

BETTY. Have some of your lovely casserole, Lynne — might settle you down a bit.

LYNNE. I doubt it, it's had tulip bulbs in it. I've sieved most of them out, now.

BETTY. Have a glass of water then, Lynne.

LYNNE. No, it'll wear off in a minute. It's only because I'm pregnant.

BETTY. Oh, that's nice — is it?

LYNNE. S' all right.

KEV. You never told me.

LYNNE. You never asked me. It'd have to run on a battery before you'd take an interest.

BETTY. Well, you won't catch me tossing the first pebble, Lynne.

LYNNE. Ta.

BETTY. You see, today's young, they don't comprehend the meaning of home entertainment Maurice — they turn to each other's private parts out of sheer boredom. In my day, it wasn't remotely the same. I kept myself happy for years with a couple of bobbins and a crochet hook. If only the council would provide adequate facilities for evening classes, we could cut down unnecessary coupling by fifty per cent.

Sings:

Handicrafts

Where is the pleasure
In days of leisure —
You soon feel flat and bored.
Life becomes fizzy,
When you get busy,
Work is its own reward.

At first it seems appealing
Staring at the ceiling,
But when hubby leaves, you soon feel blue.

If you don't want a job, be
Smart and get a hobby,
There's so many things to do.

Handicrafts can save your life,
Get a bit of lino and a Stanley knife,
Some fur fabric, kapok and foam,
You'll be happy stuffing pandas till the cows come
    home.
Glue foreign stamps on old lampshades,
Make a model of the QE2 from hearing-aids,
With some heather and a feather and some bits
    of chamois leather,
You'll be happy as the day is long.

Exercise can cheer you up,
If you want a smaller bottom or a larger cup,
The classes are easy, the only thing that's
    hard
Is trying to spend a penny in your leotard.
Learn disco-dancing if you dare,
Some ladies bring their heart pills in a
    Tupperware.
Do the Spanish Hustle, get some muscle on your
    bustle,
Just boogie now and come on strong.

Dance.

There's always Art, I'm glad to say.
Call everything a collage and you're well away,
Write a book, a play or a show,
Or an article on dishcloths, if it's what
    you know.
Learn an instrument, play some lovely tunes,
You're never alone with a pair of spoons,
Get your stretch-pants round a cello — not too
    mellow? — paint it yellow,
Be creative and you can't go wrong.

I hope I've been of use to you,
There's so many things that you can do,

Ways and means with white of egg,
Modelling support hose for the larger leg.
When your family's bored, the time won't pass,
Do something rather clever with a bunch of grass,
Sing the hard bits from La Bohéme,
And then show them your new poem,
You'll be glad you heard my little song.

KEV. I thought you were on the Pill.

LYNNE. I came off it, it made me depressed.

BETTY. Say what you like, you don't get depressed with a sheath.

LYNNE. I do.

KEV. How much pregnant are you?

LYNNE. I don't know — what difference does it make to you?

KEV. Well, it's my baby, isn't it? Isn't it?

LYNNE. Oh yeah.

KEV. I love babies, me. I can get it some boxing gloves. Hey, it can play with my Scalextric. We can have speed trials. We'd better fix a wedding, hadn't we, or something?

LIZ *comes out of the bathroom.*

LYNNE. We're not getting married. I'm giving the baby to Liz, aren't I, Liz?

LIZ. Yes, lovely. I can't wait.

BETTY. Oh, lovely ankle socks Liz, haven't you got nice sturdy legs.

LIZ. Did Mike come back up?

BETTY. Who's Mike? I do hate that shortening. Michael's such a lovely name.

LIZ. He's one of our star attractions. He's doing the Punch and Judy.

BETTY. Oh, yes. I'm looking forward to that. I love it when he throws the baby out.

LIZ. That's because you've suppressed your own urges to batter your child, and your guilt finds release in laughter.

BETTY. Well, I laugh when he steals the sausages, too. What's your explanation for that?

LIZ. Penis envy.

BETTY. It's an ugly word, envy.

KEV. What do you mean, Liz is having it? It's mine.

LYNNE. It's nothing to do with you. Liz has been explaining it to me — I'm my own person. Anyway, science is making intercourse obsolete, thank Christ. If there was a sperm bank near here, I'd have opened an account by now.

KEV. But I thought we were going to get married, and have a flat, and have our mates round and stuff.

LYNNE. Liz says marriage is stultifying.

KEV. You know I don't know what that means, you're just trying to make me look stupid.

LYNNE. You just want an unpaid servant, you.

KEV. I don't. I love you. If you think all them things about me, I'll get out of your way.

He kicks the booth down, and leaves.

LYNNE. I'll talk him round later. He gets upset a lot when there's no football.

BETTY. Put another cassette on Maurice.

Enter ELSIE.

LIZ. Are the ankle socks all right? Does it all work?

ELSIE. I've just seen Kev crying, what happened?

LIZ. Oh, nothing. (*They go through to the room.*) He's not intelligent enough to bring up a baby.

ELSIE. No, people should be sterilised if they've got less than five 'O' levels.

LIZ. Are you drunk?

ELSIE. Well, it doesn't take much with me, you know. Two Lucozades and a Junior Aspirin, and I'm doing the hokey-cokey in a shower cap.

She pours out drinks all round. Focuses on BETTY *and*
LYNNE, *who are doing the roly-poly together.*

Morning.

BETTY. Elsie, have you had a liquid lunch?

ELSIE. Yes, I ran my sandwiches under the cold tap. I love this
music.

BETTY. Just putting myself in the mood for my solo.

ELSIE. What are you going to wear?

BETTY. Do you want to see?

ELSIE. Yeah.

BETTY. Do you really?

ELSIE. Yeah, come on.

BETTY. Turn your backs, boys.

*She slips out of her trouser suit, to reveal her outfit — all
worst fears realised. She keeps on her hush-puppies.*

Daddy, darling could you? Thank you. What we did before the
zip I shall never know. Mind my puppies. I bet you never knew
they did support hose in lurex. Did you? I surprised Daddy
with my new cossy the other day — jumped out on him
while he was shaving — boo; he was thrilled weren't you lamb?
Ole! I shall be making up later. We do disco eye shadow now
you know.

LYNNE. Do you? I might get some of that.

BETTY. Do, I can probably get you some damaged — or if there's
none damaged I'll damage some. How about you, Gail?

GAIL. I'm afraid I don't go in for discotheques, personally.

BETTY. However do you spend your evenings, then?

GAIL. Marking, ironing my overall — a dedicated teacher can
always find something to do.

BETTY. No young men, then?

GAIL. Well, there's no male teachers at my school, except Mr Sloman in Biology. Not only does he reck of formaldehide, but he's a homosexual.

BETTY. Lovely.

GAIL. Fortunately, I'm broadminded about sexual deviancy. If men want to fiddle about with each other's backsides, let them. Cheers.

BETTY. Let them eat cake. (*The wine is very potent.*) Maurice, we've forgotten the H.T.'s. (*Whispers to nearest person.*) Hedge-trimmers.

MAURICE. Eh? What is the woman going on about?

BETTY. The H.T.'s — to T. the H. with. For the party.

MAURICE. Heavens, yes. It's still on the roofrack.

BETTY. The H.T.'s?

MAURICE. No, the bloody H. I'd better get it, you never know in a place like this.

BETTY. Perhaps you should have a quick practice downstairs, as well.

MAURICE (*as they leave*). I've been doing it ever since we moved out of mother's.

BETTY. True. But not to music. Back soon, Liz, pet.

LIZ. I'm going to see if Mike's in the Salad Bar.

She leaves. LYNNE *and* ELSIE *are knocking back the wine. So are* GAIL *and* FRANK, *who are snuggling up over 'Eighty English Folk Songs'*

FRANK. It's not often I get to make sandwiches with a girl like you. I thought it worked jolly well, me scraping it on . . .

GAIL. And me scraping it off.

FRANK (*sings*).

Frank and Gail Duet

You know I think you're rather nice
I expect that you're admired by thousands of chaps

I've nearly tried to kiss you twice,
When I look at you
I want to do
Something crazy, perhaps
Though I can't actually think of anything in
   particular at the moment.

GAIL.
   With me I think you could do worse
   I'm known at school for being fair but firm
   I don't smoke, I don't mislay my purse.
   I'm eight stone ten,
   I don't see men
   During the term.
   I don't go out with them in the holidays either.

BOTH.
   If you're feeling lenient
   It would be quite convenient
   To try and fall in love.

FRANK. You've got a bit of ham on your stocking, or tight I
   should say.

   Sings.

   I confess I've been involved before
   With what can only be described as a bird
   She lured me to the second floor
   And in the gloom
   Of the bindings room
   French kissing occurred
   And then fortunately somebody came in.

BOTH.
   Perhaps some day or another
   When I've checked with my mother
   We could fall in love.

GAIL. Can you foxtrot?

FRANK. Afraid not. Can you?

GAIL. No. Only Israeli.

FRANK (*sings*).

The world's our oyster

GAIL.

We could go to Perth.
I'll stuff your eggs

FRANK.

And I'll change your plugs

BOTH.

We'll spend our evenings watching *Life on Earth*
We'll play Tiddleywinks
Drink milky drinks
From His and Hers mugs.

GAIL. I wonder if they do them with Frank and Gail on them . . .

FRANK. I say, it's a good job you're not called Stein.

GAIL. Why?

They go into the toilet.

LYNNE. This whole place is barmy if you ask me. I either spend all day pissing about with chives, or painting the eyelids of that Indian bloke on the double doors of the Corn Exchange.

ELSIE. Ghandi?

LYNNE. Omar Sharif. He's right overrated, him.

ELSIE. Ghandi?

LYNNE. Omar Sharif. Is he the one that doesn't eat nothing?

ELSIE. Omar Sharif?

LYNNE. Ghandi.

ELSIE. He doesn't eat a lot, no, he's dead.

LYNNE. No wonder he likes him, then.

ELSIE. Who?

LYNNE. My dad. He likes dead people, my dad. Winston Churchill, people like that. (*Pause.*) I'd never seen cloves till

I come here. I put them in everything now. They're in that stew.

ELSIE. Out of a screw-top jar?

LYNNE. That's right.

ELSIE. Carpet tacks.

LYNNE. The doctor said I needed more iron in my diet.

The phone rings.

ELSIE. That'll be the phone.

ELSIE *goes to answer the phone.*

ELSIE. (*into phone*). OK. . . . It's behind the main Arts Centre, the old building, red door. See you soon. Bye. (*Goes back to* LYNNE.) You'd better go through the stew with a magnet.

LYNNE. Why?

ELSIE. That was the cystitis woman. She says three hundred of them are marching down in about twenty minutes. She says they're ravenous, and looking forward to it tremendously. (*Pours more drinks.*) I'd better go and breathe on that pig.

LYNNE. Perhaps if we hid in the toilet.

ELSIE. That's the last place to hide. (*Puts pig into sleeping-bag*)

MIKE *comes in. He stops in the doorway.*

MIKE. Liz around?

ELSIE. No.

MIKE (*comes in*). Great. Can you just tell her I've gone off this Punch and Judy thing. It's not really what I want to do any more.

ELSIE. Rightio.

MIKE. I won't stay. Don't want her getting heavy with me.

ELSIE. With you? She wouldn't get heavy with you if you cut her legs off.

MIKE. Yeah, I know. I banged her head against the side of an ice-cream van once, and as soon as she'd stopped crying, she bought me a 99.

ELSIE. Liz has got some fab news for you. The patter of tiny anoraks.

LYNNE. I'm going to play 'O will you wash my father's shirt'.

LYNNE goes to the piano and stares at it.

ELSIE. Liz is adopting Lynne's baby, so that she can come and live with you in Wales.

MIKE. Really.

Enter LIZ.

This should be interesting.

LIZ. Oh, there you are.

LYNNE starts to play 'Oh will you wash my father's shirt' on the piano.

Now, listen, I haven't quite finished the script, but don't worry about it, because I'll make sure you're on last. I've got some amazing news.

ELSIE. I've told him.

LIZ. Isn't it great? So I'll see you in about seven months' time, me and the baby with our wellies on, in — what's the name of the place the village?

MIKE. It hasn't got a name.

LIZ. Sorry, I know things like that are irrelevant. I know it's on a ley-line, anyway.

MIKE. It doesn't exist. I made it up.

LIZ. The village?

MIKE. The commune. The field. The tepees. The mortgage.

LIZ. What's the money been going on, then?

MIKE. A new Dormobile. Hire purchase.

LIZ. None of it was real?

MIKE. No.

Pause.

LIZ. That's fine. It was very imaginative. A sort of living theatre thing. What made you think of tepees?

MIKE. I saw a documentary on television. You don't mind?

Pause.

LIZ. No, I think it's very healthy that you can act out your fantasies in that way. Also, I feel very proud that you were able to tell me about it. I think it's a big step forward in our relationship.

ELSIE gets up and walks to the door. A hedge is thrown through the doorway. LYNNE comes over to look at it.

BETTY (*off*). Can somebody catch that? I've just dropped the trimmers!

MAURICE (*entering*). All these flipping sockets are round pin, now where's that screwdriver . . . (*Goes into kitchen.*)

BETTY (*entering*). Michael! Liz, this is my son. Give me a big kiss.

LYNNE. I'm going to be sick. (*Heads for the bathroom.*)

ELSIE. So is Liz.

BETTY. I didn't think he'd got my message, but here he is, Geography teacher extraordinaire.

LYNNE. Frank's giving Gail one up against the geyser. (*Rushes out.*)

ELSIE. He isn't.

LYNNE. No, I made it up.

BETTY. Daddy, the boy's here.

MAURICE. Is he? Has he brought my saw back?

BETTY. Manners darling; say hello to the girls.

MIKE. Hi.

BETTY. Michael, where do you learn these words? Something else you picked up in group therapy, I suppose. It's best to be open about it — my son's not been well, trouble between the ears, wasn't it, darling? Still, mental illness is nothing to go mad about these days, is it?

LIZ. I've known loads of mentally-ill people, and they were all really nice.

MIKE. What was your message again, Mummy?

BETTY. Well, Liz, here is having a little party here today.

ELSIE. Three hundred people. The woman rang up. They'll be on their way soon.

BETTY. Big audience for you, darling. We thought you could do your impressions, and some lovely folk-songs, be like old times. You're lucky to have him Liz, they're all off to Redcar next week. This silly one sold the bungalow at the end of last term, they've been homeless all summer practically. Some peculiar person Michael met lent them a flat. Practically a slum and she's charging them a fortune. Now why don't you get into a huddle with Liz, sort yourselves out while I hear Daddy's joke (*To* ELSIE:) Come through pet, he's bound to get it all bottom to sideways and we shall have a few less darns and beggars if there's a witness.

They go into the kitchen.

MIKE. Anything you want to say before I go?

LIZ. Just that if you haven't hired a removal van yet I get on really well with the girls at Hertz.

MIKE (*leaving*). Say goodbye to Mummy for me.

LIZ. Look, I don't have to dress like this if that's what's putting you off.

MIKE. I'm sorry I'm not with you.

LIZ. This is your chameleon speaking, I'll change to suit you. If you want to be an artist or whatever, I'll help you. And if you want me to be middle class,

Sings:

I'll Do Anything

It's simple to arrange,
I only have to change,
Live a different life,

As a teacher's wife.
I'll do anything,
Go and live in Tring,
Learn enamelling,
I don't care what I do, 'cos I'll do it for you.

I'll build houses,
Wear Littlewood's blouses,
Learn the names of Yorkshire's bowlers,
Wear Carmen rollers,
Learn where blusher goes,
Wash between my toes,
Never pick my nose,
I could do you proud, if I was allowed.

I'm sorry my figure's so bad,
I get my bottom half from my Mum.
But Marks and Spencers sell these sort of strong
    knicker things
That are supposed to hold up your bum.
Won't watch *Sooty* or *The Incredible Hulk*
I will buy all my lavatory paper in bulk.
I'll be a knitter and jumper unraveller,
Shop once a week in a white Morris Traveller.
We'll have solid fuel,
And a power tool
And a new kagool,
One for me, one for you, one orange, one blue.

I know my ship will come in
Once you are at my helm
And I'll learn sexual technique
From a series in *Woman's Realm*.

Life with me could be a riot,
I'll learn to strip pine, and go on a diet.
We'll have children called Mathew and Lionel
I'll use two deodorants — plain and vaginal.
Just want to be with you,
Agree with you,
Kiss and hug with you.

   Make a rug with you,
   Be snug with you,
   Be smug with you,
   For the rest of my life.
   Could you get rid of your wife?

MIKE. No, I couldn't, all right?

LIZ. Fine. I'm sure she's a really nice person. I bet I'd get on really well with her. Perhaps I should move to Redcar, and we could do all that middle-class adultery bit, twice a week at my flat when she thinks you're at squash.

MIKE. I would be at squash if I was up you. I bet it's cavernous. I bet it's like putting your cock up the Bermuda Triangle. I worked bloody hard for those cheques, but there are limits. (*Leaving.*) You needn't try and cancel the last cheque, cashed it at the Co-Op Bank this morning. We'll be out of the flat in an hour, we're having a week's holiday before term starts. A luxury caravan outside Aberystwyth. Take care.

 He leaves. MAURICE *comes into the office.*

MAURICE. Oh, I thought Michael was here — beg your pardon.

LIZ. He's just gone.

MAURICE. Didn't have a saw with him, did he?

LIZ. No.

MAURICE. Coming back, is he?

LIZ. I don't think so.

MAURICE. I'm not surprised, he's as mad as a hatter — always has been. I think he's a nancy boy, no two ways about it. Blown a hole in your cabaret, though, hasn't it? Dear me, yes. Pity you never saw him do his Shirley Abicair, very good. (*Goes back into room.*) I should cancel, if I were you, there won't be any lighting, I'll tell you that for nothing. Betty! The Boy's gone again.

 LIZ *follows him into the room.*

BETTY. Oh, no.

MAURICE. Gets that from your side of the family.

BETTY. I'm sorry, Liz, he's like this, unpredictable. Oh well . . .

Enter LYNNE.

LYNNE. What's up?

BETTY. My son's had to cancel. Personal problems.

LIZ. Let's not get despondent. How's everything else getting on?

BETTY. Well, we're pretty well set up, now, I think. Though how we're going to manage without Michael, I dread to think. I could extend my solo, perhaps bring in the Kung Fu. (*Attempts a Kung Fu disco dance step*)

MAURICE. Oh, please, no.

BETTY. Oh, shut up, that bookcase has always been wobbly. Could you do a bit more, Maurice?

MAURICE. Well, crikey, I can't trim two hedges, can I? I'm not sure this one will replant as it is.

LIZ. Well, the cassette's working at least.

MAURICE. God knows how, the bloody plugs are shot through, if you'll pardon my French.

He kicks the plug, blows a fuse, the record-player stops.

LIZ. Can you fix that, do you think?

MAURICE. Oh, yes, I'll cure cancer and arrange for World Peace at the same time, shall I? (*Flicking light switch.*) Can't turn the trimmers on now, can we?

LIZ. Would scissors be any use? Did you get the duet sorted out?

ELSIE. I don't know. Gail!

Doorbell.

LIZ. Granary Annexe. Hold on, I'll come down.

GAIL *emerges from the loo, flushed and crumpled.* FRANK *follows in the same condition.*

ELSIE. What have you been doing?

GAIL. Just explaining the ins and outs of Lattice Jam Tart.

ELSIE. Did you get that music?

GAIL. No. The cooker's not working. Has the electricity gone off?

ELSIE. Some of it.

GAIL. I don't think this will be very appetising when it cools down.

LYNNE. It was bad enough when it was hot.

FRANK. Gail's sandwiches are rather amazing. (*Indicates two small plates full.*)

LYNNE. There's three hundred people coming.

Pause.

BETTY. Well, what do you think girls?

ELSIE. It's a cock-up.

LIZ *comes back in with a telegram.*

LIZ. It's been cancelled!

ELSIE. You're joking.

BETTY. The Party?

LIZ. Yes. Unforeseen circumstances. (*Passes it round.*)

GAIL. Who's it from?

LIZ. It just says 'Organiser'. I suppose Eleanor told someone to send it.

MAURICE. Odd they didn't phone.

LIZ. Probably too embarrassed, after all the preparations.

LYNNE (*picking up stew*). Right, this is going back to the sewers.

GAIL. Drinks all round?

LIZ. Drink it all, eat the sandwiches.

ELSIE *lets the balloons down.*

ELSIE. It worked.

FRANK. Perhaps we could have the Liquorice Allsorts now, could we?

LIZ. Anything.

LYNNE *is in the bathroom. Everyone else sits down, eating and drinking.*

ELSIE. I like the black ones best, but not the coconut.

BETTY. I don't mind the coconut, but I prefer the square ones. Maurice will only eat the black and brown ones, he thinks any other shade is effeminate.

ELSIE. Who likes the black ones with the white middle? (*Everyone says they do.*) Give us the breadknife, I'll slice it up.

BETTY. Lynne was telling me, Liz, how she had an accidental fertilisation during *The Waltons.* You're very lucky to be getting the baby, it's almost impossible to adopt these days, unless you're prepared to take someone older, or coloured.

ELSIE. People are waiting years, and then being offered Oscar Peterson.

LYNNE *comes out* — LIZ *goes up to her and takes her aside.*

LIZ. Oh, Lynne — what I said before about having your baby. It's off, I'm afraid, change of plan. OK.? If it's not too late for an abortion, any help I can be with bureaucracy, let me know — I'm here to help, all right?

She joins the others as ELSIE *is slicing a Liquorice Allsort into four.*

I like those.

ELSIE. Tough.

LYNNE (*sings*).

Bloody Clowns

This is the moment
When the lights go down
I hope you're not expecting
A song about clowns.
I hate bloody clowns
And people eating fire
So you won't get nothing clever
About glitter and the old high wire.

I admit I was expecting
Things to go wrong.
I'm that sort of person
And it's that sort of song.
Who needs a circus
When you're in a mess?
I couldn't care less.

There's no Father Christmas,
It's your Dad in his socks,
Pissing about with a Selection Box.
There's no happy family
As seen on TV.
It's all slamming doors and screaming rows,
Well, it was for me.

There's no young love
No hand-in-hand
No sad sunsets
Barefoot in the sand.
None of this I love you,
Crazy about you, Lynne.
Just — my mates bet me
You won't let me put it in
Let me put it in
Let me put it in

Oh, what a fool, what a fool
To take a woman for a friend.
All that arm-in-arm laughing
Is all pretend.
She didn't help me
Who else is there to tell?
There's only me left
I don't get on with myself too well.
But I'm not bothered
I'm not bothered
Don't feel sorry for me because I don't care.

*At the end of the song, sitting away from the others, she
starts to swallow paracetamols with her wine.*

MAURICE. I tell you one thing, I'm not sorry not to be telling that darn story.

BETTY. Nor me, you've never got it right yet.

MAURICE. Well, we're spared your dancing, anyway. You were putting up the damn premium on the House Insurance.

BETTY. Button your lip, Baldy, we wanted new glass in those French Windows anyway. Novelty hedge-trimming! The novelty is if you can tell what it's meant to be. You should see the peacock by the front gate.

MAURICE. It's like a damn ferret.

ELSIE. This is a brill sandwich. Three cheers for Gail!

LIZ. Oh, yes, thanks, Gail — I hope you haven't had too bad a time.

GAIL. Oh, no, I've met some nice people, and after a little pep-talk from Elsie, I've performed my first practical joke.

LIZ. Well done. What?

GAIL. I sent that telegram.

Pause.

ELSIE. You're joking.

GAIL. No, I was when I sent it. I'm not now.

FRANK. I think it's jolly funny. Gail told me about it in the lavatory. Your face is a picture, Liz.

GAIL *and* FRANK *prepare to leave.*

LIZ. But, I want you to do the Punch and Judy please.

FRANK. Oh, no, thank you very much. I'm taking Gail to the library. I'm going to show her the computer.

GAIL. It sounds fascinating.

They leave. We hear their voices down the stairs, and then, faintly, a procession approaching.

FRANK. The Spinners are on the BBC tonight.

GAIL. They're very amusing.

Pause.

BETTY. I better not have this sandwich.

LYNNE. I've just done a silly thing.

BETTY. I think we all have.

LYNNE. I've just taken some Paracetamol.

ELSIE. How many?

LYNNE. Half a bottle — with this wine.

BETTY *jumps up — steps into her trouser suit.*

BETTY. Maurice, go down and get the car started.

MAURICE *leaves.*

Get Lynne's jacket, Elsie.

ELSIE. Shall I ring the hospital?

BETTY. No, we can be there in two minutes. Come along, Lynne, and don't worry. If you could pack up the cassette Elsie, Maurice can collect it later.

BETTY *and* LYNNE *leave.*

ELSIE. Why did she do that?

LIZ. Oh, I suppose it was because I told her I didn't want the baby. Silly cow.

ELSIE. When did you tell her that?

LIZ. Just now. (*Laughing.*) God, can you hear them singing? I haven't a clue how to put this booth up, have you? If I get some batteries, Betty can still do her dance, they'll come back, won't they? What's up? Overdoses are nothing — they've got stomach pumps and things, she won't have had time to digest them. They'll be at the hospital by now.

ELSIE. You don't know that. They could be stuck in the traffic waiting for your parade to go by.

LIZ. Perhaps.

ELSIE. I thought your big thing was being a nice person.

LIZ (*sings*).

Good Fun

Looked in the mirror aged about fourteen,
Could not aspire to third-rate beauty queen,
Got into being nice and all that stuff.
I think I've just decided that I've had enough.

Been a good listener for ten long years,
A wind-up doll with sympathetic ears,
Got mildewed shoulders from my sad friend's tears —
Well, I'm nobody's mother,
Let them stupefy each other,
Cos from now it's going to be all good fun.

For far too long, I've had an open door
To welcome what we're not supposed to call the poor.
They called me Lizzie, but not any more —
Though their hearts they may be pure in,
The deprived all stink of urine,
And my heart is only in fun — good fun for me.

I always envied you your attitude,
For your policy of 'what the hell'.
Being selfish works for you.
It can work for me as well.

I've licked the arses of the very old —
They loved me for it, I was often told.
Happy in the knowledge they would soon be cold,
I kept going till my hat trick,
My third dead geriatric —
So from now it's going to be all good fun.

What I told you of my sex life was not quite
    correct.
It's been busy, but there's not a lot that you'd
    respect.
I've laid beneath the lunatic, the sick, the wrecked —
Does it count, sex with a write-off?
With your clothes on, with the light off?
Well, who cares? From now it is all good fun
    for me.

I've always hated you, you break my rules
About the things an ugly girl should do.
You never do fuck-all for nobody —
Why do so many people fancy you?

And you expect me to feel bad for Lynne,
And blame myself now for the state she's in
I don't care who's lost, as long as I can win.
You won't catch me crying
Cos some scrubber might be dying.
I don't care, I care about me, good fun for me.

As she sings, the lights fade. ELSIE *leaves unnoticed before the last verse.* LIZ *is alone in the spotlight.*

At the end of the song, the lighting returns to normal. The procession is just outside. There is a ring on the doorbell.

Pat and Margaret

To Margaret, Ruth, Gavin, Robyn and the cast and crew of
Pat and Margaret, *with thanks*

Pat and Margaret was first shown on BBC TV in
September 1994 with the following cast:

MARGARET	Victoria Wood
PAT	Julie Walters
CLAIRE	Celia Imrie
BILLY	Don Henderson
STELLA	Deborah Grant
JIM	Duncan Preston
BELLA	Lynda Rooke
SUE	Jan Alphonse
DAISY	Amanda Pointer
JIM'S MOTHER	Thora Hird
MAEVE	Anne Reid
HELPER IN OLD AGE HOME	Julie Hesmondhalgh
OLD LADY IN HOME	Gabrielle Blunt
MARTIN, *warm-up man*	Philip Lowrie
PORTER	Charles Pemberton
VERA, *in home*	Joane Hall
VERA	Shirley Stelfox
PETE	Robert Kingswell
NADIA	Sue Wallace
BUSYBODY	Frances Cox
MR SCRUTON	Adam Warner
HOTEL MANAGER	Roger Brierley
EMMA-LOUISE	Gemma Wardle
FIRST LADY IN MOTEL	Madge Hindle
SECOND LADY IN MOTEL	Angela Curran
MR LLOYD	Tenniel Evans
SPOTTY BOY	Corrin Helliwell
STRINGER	Peter Lorenzelli
FIRST FAN	Helen Lindsay
SECOND FAN	Vera Jakob
TEA BAR LADY	Jeillo Edwards
MARGARET, *aged two*	Melissa Allen
PAT, *aged seven*	Sammy-Jo Smith

Producer Ruth Caleb
Director Gavin Millar
Production Designer Ken Starkey
Costume Designer Anna Stubley

The M6 motorway. The traffic churns by. At the Kirkby Preston Motorway Service Area All-Day Breakfast counter, MARGARET tips out her last tin of chips and clocks off. At the entrance to the locker-room her workmates are waiting for her, all dressed up. BELLA and SUE follow her into the locker-room as she takes off her uniform.

BELLA. Come on woman, got a blooming coach revving up outside.

MARGARET. No, I were waiting for chips.

BELLA. Waiting for chips. Blooming live television show to get to, she's waiting for chips.

MARGARET. Well I was.

BELLA. Well I was she says. Women! Come on!

   MARGARET scrambles into a smartish top. She still has her flat work shoes on.

BELLA. You're not going in those shoes?

MARGARET. They're comfy.

   BELLA manages to get the women moving.

SUE. Leave her alone, she'll only be sat in the audience, she's not Dame Bloody Kiri Te Sodding Kanawa.

   BELLA hustles them outside and on to the coach. MARGARET stops to talk to JIM, her boyfriend.

MARGARET. Bella's still got a ticket. Could you not come?

JIM. Better not. My mother and so forth.

MARGARET. Oh well. Where are you mopping, Gents?

JIM. There's been an overflow, Level Two urinals Southbound. They bleeped me over from Northbound.

MARGARET. You're in demand with that mop.

JIM. We have it to do.

MARGARET. So is that all right then, picking us up after?

JIM. Roger wilco, I'll be there.

BELLA (*calling from the coach*). Mrs Woman, get on!

MARGARET. Well I might be too famous to talk to you by then!

JIM. Oh, what, the telly?

MARGARET. See ya!

> MARGARET *boards the coach.* JIM *gazes after her. The door shuts and the engine starts.* JIM *mouths through the window.*

JIM. What's it called?

MARGARET. Pardon?

BELLA. Speak up Rambo!

JIM. The television – business – what's it called?

> *Everyone sings out, to the famous TV signature tune:*

ALL. *Magic Moments!*

> *The coach pulls away, to a cheer from the women.*

1958. A street of grey pebble-dashed council houses. PAT, *aged seven, parades up the street in a skimpy ruched swimming-costume, sunglasses, beads and her mother's high heels.* MARGARET, *aged two, watches from her tricycle, holding an ice-cream.* PAT *clops past her and snatches up the ice-cream.* MARGARET *looks at her but doesn't say anything.*

Heathrow Airport, International Arrivals. The press are hanging around. BILLY, *a middle-aged photographer, looks up and puts his liquorice allsorts away.*

BILLY. Sweets away, boys, get flashing.

   Up sweeps PAT, *gleaming, groomed and glamorous, surrounded by a bevy of airline officials, and* CLAIRE, *her very pregnant forty-year-old PA.* CLAIRE *is holding* PAT's *bag, make-up case, coat and flowers. The press break into a chorus of:*

PRESS. Over here, Miss Bedford.
One for me, Miss Bedford. (*Etc., etc.*)

   PAT *carefully favours each camera while giving the impression of keeping moving. She takes from* CLAIRE *a copy of her book* My Life in 'Glamor' *and poses with it.*

PAT. Really boys, you're very naughty, I know I'm going to be on the front page of every paper tomorrow looking a complete don't know what!

BILLY. Good to be back, Pat?

PAT (*sweeping away*). I'm English darling, this is home – football, Marmite, the Queen Mum . . . (*Her smile drops as she leaves the press behind.*) . . . filth, beggars, no choice of lettuce . . .

Peacock Studios. Our coach pulls up outside and the girls spill out. BELLA *tries to check them as they mill about.* MARGARET *wanders off to admire the scene.*

BELLA. Now everybody's to stick with me. We've to queue at Door 4. Where's Margaret gone now? Margaret!

   MARGARET *turns and smiles and is seized by an irate* BELLA.

BELLA. Will you stick to the party, lady!

MARGARET. I'm just looking out for celebrities.

BELLA. Don't show me up, come on.

MARGARET. This is great, isn't it?

BELLA. Yes, it's fandabidozie. Come on!

A corridor. Peacock Studios. BELLA'*s girls head the* Magic
Moments *queue. The queue is mainly composed of middle-aged and
elderly women. The girls stare at the huge framed photos on the walls.*

MARGARET. Is that Michael Barrymore?

SUE. What are you like? That's him off news. Michael
Barrymore!

   DAISY, *a young researcher with a clipboard, has a quick word
with the security man and approaches the queue.*

DAISY. Party leader? Mrs Franklyn?

BELLA. This is my party.

DAISY. Could I have a word?

   The girls pull faces at each other.

SUE. What do you bet we've got wrong tickets.

MARGARET. We haven't have we?

SUE. Or not enough – they're saying ·· everyone except her in
t'anorak.

MARGARET. They are not.

DAISY (*to* BELLA). No, that's fine. We just needed to know
she was actually on the premises.

BELLA. No, that were plain sailing, really.

DAISY. Is she the little dark one?

BELLA. No, the one in blue, with the perm.

DAISY. Oh.

BELLA. Why?

DAISY. No, I mustn't say, really I mustn't say a word.

Heathrow Arrivals. PAT *stands on the travelator, her entourage behind her. Two lady* FANS *run alongside the travelator, handing out albums of photos and autograph books.*

FIRST FAN. Miss Bedford, Miss Bedford! We wrote to you in LA! We're the two diabetics from Ketteridge!

PAT. Pen!

CLAIRE *hands over a pen.*

SECOND FAN. We won't be back in time for *Magic Moments* but we're taping it. We've ordered the book.

PAT. Sweet of you.

FIRST FAN. We never miss *Glamor.* I was once mistaken for you at a traffic-light.

PAT. Oh.

SECOND FAN. Is it true they're going to axe the series?

PAT. No.

FIRST FAN (*holding out large envelope*). Would it be possible to have a twelve-by-eight colour portrait to Kay and Bunty?

PAT. Claire.

CLAIRE *takes the envelope. The fans fall behind a little.*

FIRST FAN. Good luck with *Magic Moments*!

SECOND FAN. We loved you in *Lakeland Vet.*

FIRST FAN. We do your workout!

SECOND FAN. Do you have any message for diabetics?

They fall behind, panting.

PAT. When you deal with me, Claire, think icon.

The Magic Moments *studio. Most of the audience is seated.* BELLA's *party file into their seats, helped by an usher.* MARGARET *is about three seats in from the aisle. The floor manager nods in response to a message in his earpiece and goes to rearrange them, putting* MARGARET *on the aisle.*

SUE. Blimey, what does it matter, they're not numbered seats.

A dressing room, Peacock Studios. PAT *sweeps in with* CLAIRE, *snatches the make-up case and plonks it down on the counter in front of* NADIA, *the make-up girl.*

NADIA. Sorry, what do you want me to do with this?

PAT. Put it on me.

An office in a newspaper building, that evening. STELLA, *a glamorous fiftyish journalist, all big hair and bracelets, is setting her video with a bar-code scanner. On one wall is a poster plugging* STELLA *as Columnist of the Year. There is also a framed book cover, the back of which is a photo of* STELLA; *the front says 'Life in the Shadows, the unauthorised biography of Cliff Richard'. She speaks into a little tape recorder.*

STELLA. Yes – idea for Pat Bedford book, chapter four. Maybe analyse a typical interview, like the *Magic Moments*, break it down for grammar, vocabulary, content, really try and expose the ignorant little tart beneath the veneer.

PAT's *dressing-room.* PAT *is having her make-up touched up by* NADIA. CLAIRE *stands close by.*

NADIA. Have you seen *Magic Moments*, Miss Bedford?

PAT. No. (*To* CLAIRE's *stomach.*) Could you move that?

CLAIRE. Sorry. I had a scan today. (*She thrusts the photo in front of* PAT.) You can see his spine.

PAT. I don't care if you can see the washing instructions on his underpants. Do the job. Not interested.

NADIA. This is gorgeous powder, Miss Bedford. I don't know this brand.

PAT. I have it specially blended for me in Vagina – Geneva.

JIM's house. An extremely neat and tidy living-room. His MUM is stuffing a knitted animal with kapok. JIM is hovering about.

MUM. What's the matter with you, stop looming!

JIM. Will you be having the television on at all?

MUM. When I've stuffed this penguin to my own satisfaction, possibly.

The Magic Moments *studio. Camera are moving into position. MARTIN, the dapper warm-up man, is roaming up and down aisles with his hand-held radio mike, jollying everyone up.*

MARTIN. I think I'll come down here now, I'm fed up with you lot! Only kidding, you're a marvellous bunch. All righty, where's our party from the Chestnuts Home for the Elderly, Washwood Heath?

There's a cheer from a group of old ladies.

And we have a Mrs Maisie Stephenson, she's ninety-two years young today! Whoo!

Cheers and applause.

She's sitting over there with her mum and dad! No, only kidding, that's marvellous.

Old folks' home, Lancashire. A helper pushes a row of old ladies into position in front of the TV.

HELPER. Are you going to watch it, Vera? This is the programme Aggie was going to be on if she hadn't have died.

A corridor outside the Magic Moments *studio. PAT in full slap and costume, pacing up and down, rehearsing her anecdotes. CLAIRE stands by with PAT's paraphernalia.*

PAT. And this is another story I tell in the book – when I was invited to the Emmys, and I wore a dress that was so tight, you could see me changing my mind. The dress was so tight Maeve – you could see me changing my mind!

Round the corner at full pelt comes MAEVE, *also in full slap but with curlers and trainers, followed by* DAISY, *holding* MAEVE's *evening shoes.* PAT *and* MAEVE *kiss, without touching.*

MAEVE. Pat! You look fabulous! Was the flight OK? Are you worn out? You'll have to give me your diet, I'm getting like an old washerwoman here.

PAT. Well, it's all in my book!

MAEVE. That's great. I'll get my head combed out and I'll catch you on set later. It's a bundle of fun – it goes like a rocket. You look gorgeous. (*She bustles away and murmurs to* DAISY.) She's getting very haggard.

Magic Moments *studio.*

MARTIN. And he said, never mind that, who bombed our chip shop? Nice one that, isn't it. (*He checks his list and moves down a few steps.*) Now. Where are the ladies of the Kirkby Preston Service Area Cafeteria Serving Staff?

BELLA's *girls cheer and wave.*

You're the girls dishing up the curly sandwiches and the old burnt bangers eh?

BELLA (*off mike*). It's very good food.

MARTIN (*points his mike at her*). What's that, my darling?

BELLA. I say it's very good food these days, Martin.

MARTIN. Slap my wrist. I know it is, my sweetheart. Only kidding. They do a marvellous job on these motorways, don't they everybody?

Back in the corridor. PAT *is in a rage.* DAISY *is caught in the crossfire.*

PAT. Do you keep all your American stars waiting in corridors? Is this how Bob Hope would be treated, or Shirley MacLaine? I am the biggest soap star on American television, do you know what I was doing last night? I was dueting, in harmony, with Liza Minnelli and Macaulay Culkin.

DAISY. Erm – sorry – it's unavoidable.

PAT. No. What's your name?

DAISY. Daisy.

PAT. No, Daisy. It's not unavoidable. There is never a good reason for malatreating a top-rated celebrity, and the sooner you get a grip on that factum, the more likely you'll do so! (*Realising there's half a sentence missing here, she snaps her fingers at* CLAIRE.) Water!

Magic Moments *studio.*

MARTIN. Well, we're nearly ready to go, let me just remind you one more time – it is a live show, we can't go back and do it again – so if you do get called out by Maeve, and this is a surprise type show, lots of we hope nice surprises in store for one or two of you – if you do get called out – just come straight down, there'll be someone to show you the way – watch your language – no effing and blinding please – no alternative comedy – not nice these days, is it – just got a minute or two to go now. Now, who remembers Lenny the Lion?

Holding area behind the Magic Moments *set.* MAEVE, *now combed out and with her high heels on, very grim and businesslike, is examining a script with* DAISY, *who holds her trainers.*

MAEVE. Yeah, OK, so we think they haven't seen each other for twenty-seven years.

DAISY. They don't look alike by the way.

MAEVE. Oh damn, that would have been nice wouldn't it. And they're moving that autocue nearer, yeah?

DAISY. Yeah.

MAEVE. How do you say this? Motters-head?

DAISY. Motter-shead I think.

MAEVE. Mottershead. Margaret Mottershead.

A floor assistant pokes her head round a flat and gives MAEVE *the thumbs up.* MAEVE *hands her glasses to* DAISY.

OK. Mottershead. Mottershead. Oh God, what's first now? The puppy!

The old folks' home. The old ladies stare at the TV as Magic Moments *begins.*

HELPER. Wake up, Vera. Pat Bedford's on this, you like her, don't you?

JIM's *living-room.* JIM *has the TV on. A lavatory flushes. On the TV screen,* MAEVE *descends a staircase to music and applause.* MUM *comes in.*

MUM. What's this? This is never wildlife of the Kalahari.

JIM. The girls from work are in the audience.

MUM (*stretching her hand out for the remote*). Don't handle this please, it's all over lavatory cleaner now.

She changes channels, the music changes to desert-type and JIM *turns away, defeated.*

The holding area. PAT *is pacing furiously and shouting at* CLAIRE. *A meek floor assistant is keeping well out of the way.*

PAT. I've been in earthquakes that were better organised than this.

CLAIRE. I think it's just that they don't want anyone in the audience to see you.

PAT. Thank you Claire. You have a lifetime's experience in show business do you? Or is getting pregnant and not tracking down the right bra it?

Magic Moments *studio.* BELLA *and her girls are applauding wildly at some sentimental item.* MAEVE *turns to her camera as an old man,* HARRY, *leading a puppy, is led off the set.*

MAEVE. Wasn't that lovely? And Harry not only gets the puppy but all that lovely dog food.

MARGARET. Ah! Any chance of me going to the toilet?

BELLA. No! Stay put!

MAEVE. Now we've had some extraordinary reunions on *Magic Moments* but I think you'll find this one is extra special. It concerns two people – one of the ladies in question thinks she's just here for a night out with the girls – the girls of the Kirkby Preston Motorway Service Area Cafeteria.

SUE, MARGARET *and the girls all look at each other.* BELLA *stares straight ahead.*

MAEVE. Yes – step into the limelight – this is your Magic Moment – Margaret Mottershead!

The girls shriek. An usher leads MARGARET *as she half stumbles down the steps to* MAEVE, *dumping her bag and anorak at the last minute.* MARTIN *keeps the applause going.* MARGARET *sits on an adjoining sofa to* MAEVE, *a monitor between them. Behind them is a huge video wall, on which we see a series of old photos.*

MAEVE. Now tell us who that is, Margaret.

MARGARET. My Aunty Aggie – she lived next door.

MAEVE. She lived next door to you and your sister. And she looked after you and minded you, whatever.

MARGARET *nods.*

Well she was a big fan of the programme.

Scattered applause.

And she had a bit of a story to tell about you and your sister. We were hoping she'd come and tell us in the studios, but she's dead unfortunately – but anyway . . .

A photo of PAT and MARGARET at the ages of six and two comes up on the screen.

There you are now. You're the little one, yes? Love those old woolly costumes don't you? And who's the big girl?

MARGARET. That's my sister Pat.

STELLA's *office. As* MARGARET *says the word 'Pat',* STELLA *is suddenly riveted to the television.*

The back of the Magic Moments *set.* PAT *is ushered by a floor assistant into the studio with* CLAIRE. *There is a monitor, which* PAT *is too busy complaining to notice.* DAISY *hurries to meet* PAT.

DAISY. Only one second now, I promise.

PAT. As soon as I get to a telephone, you're fired.

On the set. MARGARET *sits uncomprehending.*

MAEVE. Now Pat and your mammy didn't get on too well, had a bit of a row, usual thing, and off Pat heads, bright lights and all, whatever.

MARGARET *stares at her.*

And you were what, about ten at the time, and you totally lost touch, you've never seen her from that day to this. A common enough tale on *Magic Moments* but let's take a closer look at that naughty runaway sister Pat.

The back of the set. The floor assistant stands by to lead PAT *on.*

PAT. You're very fortunate I'm a consommé professional.
Mirror!

CLAIRE *hands her a mirror, she checks her cleavage and hands it back. She then notices the monitor, which shows a close-up of* PAT *aged about nine.*

On the set. MARGARET *stares at the old photo of* PAT *in a deckchair.*

MAEVE. See anybody you recognise?

The audience is baffled, but some are beginning to cotton on.

How about this?

The shot changes to a publicity photo of PAT *aged eighteen, from 1969. The audience gets very excited.*

Recognise her now?

The shot changes to PAT *as she appears in* Glamor. *The audience 'oohs' and 'aahs'.* MARGARET *is frozen.*

Yes! Margaret Mottershead, motorway waitress, the sister you haven't seen for twenty-seven years, now one of the highest paid actresses in American television – a very special Magic Moment – here she is – from *Glamor* – the glamorous – Patricia Bedford.

The audience bursts into wild applause. PAT *stands side stage, unable to believe what has happened.* MARTIN *and the floor assistant keep the applause going.*

Well I know she's here 'cos I saw her round the back when I was in me curlers. Come and meet your sister – Patricia Bedford!

PAT *stumbles on to the set as if pushed, recovers herself, takes the applause and goes to* MARGARET *with outstretched arms.* MARGARET *stands up awkwardly. They embrace.* BELLA *and the girls are overcome.*

MAEVE. Isn't that our best one yet? Well, they've an awful lot of catching up to do, which we'll find out all about next week – meanwhile, back in a couple of minutes with more Magic Moments.

The lights dim to silhouette.

MARTIN. We're off the air, folks!

MAEVE is rushed at by sound men and make-up girls. PAT and MARGARET look at each other. MARTIN is chatting to the audience.

MARGARET. Pat?

PAT (*breaking away*). Sorry, would you excuse me . . .

She turns away, leaving MARGARET on the set. The audience flood happily out to the exit. BELLA and the girls clatter down the stairs.

SUE. Did you know, you bugger?

BELLA. No, I thought she were getting a prize for chip frying or summat.

SUE. Well what now? Is there a do?

BELLA. Oh yeah, there must be. Well, we can't all – look, can you get them on the coach, just for now, and I'll go round and ask.

Hospitality – a bare, featureless conference room with a bar and buffet table set up at one end. There are a few production people, Harry and the puppy, and a couple of waitresses. BILLY, armed with his camera, is hovering hopefully by the buffet with DAISY.

DAISY. Did you get the studio shots with Pat and her sister?

BILLY. They weren't on the floor

DAISY. Well do them in here then.

BILLY. What are those then, vol au vents?

DAISY. Hands off, Billy. We don't take the clingfilm off till

Maeve comes.

MAEVE *sweeps in with her team, high on adrenalin.*

MAEVE. Well, you'll have to go a long way to beat that one.
Did you see their faces, that Margaret, I thought now please
nobody die, oh God give us a drink, hi Billy, just head and
shoulders tonight eh, I'll never get my shoes back on, it's a
pity I'm too grand to soak them in a bucket, get the clingfilm
off, let me at the chicken legs – now, what's Pat having?
Where is Pat?

*A studio corridor. PAT, thinking furiously, is led by CLAIRE to the
lifts. They pass a ladies' toilet.*

CLAIRE. Oh golly, I'm sorry, you see his back is right on my
bladder – two ticks!

   CLAIRE *nips in and* PAT *turns round and goes back to the
   studio.*

*The old folks' home. The helpers are wheeling the old ladies out. One,
VERA, is very agitated and pointing at the screen.*

HELPER. Come on Vera, coming for cocoa?

VERA. It was my Pat! My Pat!

HELPER. What say, Vera?

VERA. That was her, I recognise her now – it's my little girl!

   The helpers look at each other, not sure how to take this.

*The empty studio. MARGARET is up in the seating, collecting her
bag and brushing the dust off her anorak. PAT comes on to the
studio floor. MARGARET is thrilled.*

MARGARET. Hiya! I didn't know where everybody had gone, I
didn't know what I was supposed to do – my sister being the

one in *Glamor* -- I'm gobsmacked, me!

PAT. Come down here.

MARGARET *comes down.*

MARGARET. 'Cos you give me such a funny look before -- I had this horrible feeling – erk – she doesn't want me to be here –

PAT. I don't.

MARGARET. Pardon?

PAT. I don't want to talk to you.

MARGARET. Why not?

PAT. I don't want this. I'm doing a book. I'm here to plug a book.

MARGARET. What have I to do then?

PAT. How did you get here?

MARGARET. We came on a coach.

PAT. Fine. Go and get on it. I'll deal with everything else.

MARGARET. Do you not want to know about me?

PAT. No. I don't want to know.

MARGARET. Have I just to go then?

PAT *nods.* MARGARET *turns and plods up the steps.*

The studio coach park. The coach is full of laughing, chatting girls.
BELLA *climbs on board.*

SUE. What's happening?

BELLA. You tell me. Margaret's round the back somewhere, they wouldn't let me through.

SUE. Shall we hang on a bit for her?

BELLA. Well we can't wait long.

Studio corridor. MARGARET is lost and starting to panic. She's going along corridors, opening fire doors, wrong doors, doors she's opened before. CLAIRE comes bounding round a corner, holding a few copies of PAT's book.

CLAIRE. Hi! Coming up for a nosh?

MARGARET. Do you know where the coach would be?

CLAIRE. The coach?

MARGARET. We all came on the coach. I don't want them to leave without me.

CLAIRE. Oh no, you're staying with Pat tonight, well, for as long as –

MARGARET. Is that what Pat wants?

CLAIRE. Oh yes, I'm sure – she must be thrilled. Anyway, come on, you're missing the party!

MARGARET. Could my friends come? Would that be all right?

CLAIRE. Oh gosh yes! Ask for Hospitality, I'll see you there!

MARGARET. I'll go and get them then.

The coach park. BELLA stands on the steps of the coach, looking out over the empty park. MARGARET sees the coach from the window of the studio building and dashes down. The door is chained, and as MARGARET waves and calls, BELLA boards the coach and it pulls away.

PAT, a little more relaxed, walks to Hospitality with CLAIRE.

PAT. I get letters from people like that all the time. They're my sister, they're my mother. I'm glamorous, attractive, I have enough sexual charisma to open a factory – she's fat, Northern, working class – of course she wants to be my sister. I absolutely sympathise – life is very tough for these Northern women. I did a cameo on a Barbara Taylor Bradford – it was heartbreaking. Anyway, she's gone, no harm done – if we can just get that bit edited out, put in an interview concentrating on the book, and ooh la la.

They go through into –

Hospitality.

CLAIRE. No, she's still here – she's coming up to the party with her friends from the motorway.

PAT is greeted by MAEVE's merry group as this news sinks in.

MAEVE. Pat!

PAT is drawn into the group and given a drink.

I said, didn't I, her and that sister of hers will be having a good old natter somewhere, catching up on the old times – what a story! They had some trouble digging it up; you're as close as a clam with the old personal info – now where's the Margaret woman?

PAT. I'll just get Claire to fetch her. Excuse me a moment.

DAISY. Harry with the dog, wasn't that sweet.

They continue with the shop talk as PAT snatches her bag from CLAIRE and takes out some cash.

PAT. Stop her coming in here. Give her this and get her to go.

CLAIRE. What should I say, she was awfully thrilled. I mean I thought she seemed terribly nice.

PAT. Take it and do it. Roger! (*She turns back to the crowd.*)

An empty tea bar. Almost deserted, it's obviously not where the party is. MARGARET sits alone. A large West Indian LADY behind the till looks at her suspiciously.

TEA LADY. We don't serve you.

MARGARET. No, I'm just -- (*She straightens the salt and pepper.*) I like your till.

CLAIRE *dashes in.* MARGARET *stands up in relief.*

MARGARET. I didn't know where anybody was, I was just thinking – this probably isn't the right place is it?

CLAIRE. I've just had a wee word with Pat.

MARGARET. The coach went.

CLAIRE. She just wondered if I could give you this!

MARGARET. You see – I don't have any way of getting home now.

CLAIRE. Right.

MARGARET. So what about staying with Pat – is that still on? – otherwise I'm a bit lumbered.

CLAIRE. No, that's absolutely –

They start to move off. MARGARET *is relieved.*

MARGARET. 'Cos I don't know the set-up. I don't know Pat. I've not seen her since I was ten – there's not much in it for her, me turning up!

Hospitality.

PAT. Now I do have to go rather shortly, it's been a very long flight, and a very long day.

MAEVE. Oh God yes, understood.

PAT. And my people will be talking to your people, but I'm afraid there's been somewhat of a virago.

MAEVE. A what?

DAISY. Farrago?

MAEVE. Fandango? Façade?

PAT. The sister thing.

MAEVE. The Magic Moment?

PAT. The part where you brought on the sister – I wonder how much of an upheaval would it be to edit that part out.

MAEVE. Take your bit out?

PAT. Yes.

MAEVE. No problem. In fact, we'll give you the whole thing. Daisy would have sent you a tape anyway.

PAT. Yes, thank you – but no – I meant – take that bit out of the programme altogether – not show it.

MAEVE. Well it's a nice idea, there's lots of things I'd like to go back and do again –

PAT. Oh, so you could –

MAEVE. The nice thing about it being live, we don't have to worry about it – it's over –

PAT. It's live? It's already been out?

MAEVE. We went live in ninety-two, you have been away a long time.

CLAIRE *comes in with* MARGARET.

MAEVE. Margaret, for heaven's sake. Will you get yourself outside a glass of champagne before it all goes. Let's have a toast to sisters!

PAT *and* MARGARET. Sisters!

BILLY *snaps their pose.*

BILLY. Lovely. Any chance of a kiss?

PAT's *suite, Regent Hotel. The doors are flung open with a flourish by a* MANAGER, *followed by* PAT, *two sweating porters,* CLAIRE, MARGARET *and a publicity lady. A maid is scuttling about doing flowers etc.*

MARGARET *is drawn into the suite, which is huge and over-decorated, covered in flowers. She stands open-mouthed while* PAT *goes into overdrive. The poor maid gets drawn into it all.*

PAT. I want everything unpacked and the Chanel, the St
   Laurent and the Issey Miyake pressed immediately.
   Comprehendé? Bring them back the second the work is
   completed; as an icon, I'm very vulnerable and I don't wish
   my under or outer wear to be a target for perverts' hand relief.
   Yes? *Si*? *Oui-oui*? That lamp lit, that one dimmed, TV to
   CNN . . .

   They all scuttle round. She scans a menu.

   Four ounces of freshly squeezed organic grape juice, skinless
   chicken on granary no animal fat and an 'erb tea.

MANAGER. Anything else I can do to help, Miss Bedford?

PAT. No. Claire, drapes, close. You – put that in the bathroom
   and everyone else can leave now.

   They all disappear through various doors. MARGARET *wanders
   off to inspect the other rooms.*

PAT. Well?

CLAIRE. Er, sorry?

PAT. Thanks to your umbilical incompetence, I, sexy yet
   vulnerable, and I'm quoting from *Harper's* here, I, Pat
   Bedford, of *Glamor*, have been exposed on nationwide
   television as having some dubious connection with an
   overweight Northern waitress with all the sophisticated allure
   of an airline salad. I, who came sixth in the World's Most
   Envied Bottom poll, 1992 – only two below Claudia Schiffer –
   am now publicly linked to a woman whose buttocks practically
   skim the carpet.

CLAIRE. But she's so nice – and she's having such a lovely
   time.

PAT. I gave you fifty pounds to give her and tell her to go. Did
   you give it to her? Did she leave? No. Have I had the money
   back? No.

CLAIRE (*fumbling in her bag*). But I just kept thinking if my
   baby had a sister, and if they got separated, and if somebody
   gave my baby fifty pounds not to see my other baby –

PAT. Yes, and if I had a penis and a hairy chest I could play Hamlet, King Lear and Robin Prince of Thieves. I can't afford to have her here. You know *Glamor*'s dropped down from the top spot; any excuse, any hint of a scandal we'll be off the air, or even worse, on the air without me. I'm Valerie Lady Charleson, I'm Knightsbridge, I'm grooming, I'm camisoles. I can't be seen to have a blood relative with a Lancashire accent and a perm you could go trick-or-treating in.

CLAIRE. But I don't think she'd –

PAT. It looks wrong. It's not me. Oh – come early and help me get rid of her – before the press call.

CLAIRE. I'll . . . OK . . . I'll get a cab then . . . I think she's so nice . . .

PAT, *not listening, is changing channels and cramming grapes into her mouth.* CLAIRE *tries to leave.*

PAT. Oh and Claire – when handling drapes, don't drag them manually – it's very bad for the fabric – use the pulleys provided. (*She demonstrates.*) Like so, and so.

MARGARET *taps at an inner door and comes in, smiling.*

MARGARET. Do you knock or not, I don't know. They don't tell you that one do they, in t'magazines. Do you knock door of famous sister you haven't seen for twenty-seven years? Or do you not knock? Blooming heck though, this. I mean what is it like? There's pot-pourri on the top of the toilet in there, that would be four pounds in a shop. Even on the market that would be four pounds. And the pillows on the bed! Eight pillows! This thick! Make mine look like cream crackers! Sorry – I'm going on. It's the champagne – I could never see why they went on about it before.

PAT. I'm going to bed.

MARGARET. Yes, I'm sorry. I'm worn out and I've only come on t'motorway. I can't really phone Bella now, can I. I'll phone them at work tomorrow.

PAT. Don't call anybody.

MARGARET. Fair enough. I'll get to bed then as well. Are
them shower caps free, do you know?

PAT. Yes, it's all free.

MARGARET. Oh, terrific. Night then. Oh – the only thing is,
'cos I didn't know I was coming, I've no pants.

PAT. Pants?

MARGARET. Clean pants for tomorrow. Tights I can rinse
through –

*PAT leaves. MARGARET follows her to the doorway and takes
the tiny pair of lacy pants PAT holds out.*

Oh ta.

PAT. I have to go to bed.

MARGARET. Don't worry about what you said to me before,
about wanting me to go. I'd only come to watch the show – I
wasn't expecting blooming sister to come crawling out the
woodwork, I wasn't that thrilled myself to tell you the honest
truth. I was thinking oh blimey last time I saw her she
smacked me across the face. Do you remember?

PAT. No. Look – I must –

She starts to close the door on MARGARET.

MARGARET. Oh – what time's breakfast? What time have we
to be down by?

The door closes.

*The Kirkby Preston Motorway Services. It's late. The coach pulls up
at the Staff Entrance. BELLA and a couple of the other women
wearily get out. JIM looms up out of the shadows. BELLA walks to
her car.*

BELLA. Oh, it's you.

JIM. Wasn't Margaret being dropped off here – was that not the
arrangement?

BELLA. Did you not see it?

JIM. No, my mother wanted the wildlife.

BELLA. Yes, well she's Pat Bedford's sister seemingly.

JIM. Sorry?

BELLA. Her in *Glamor*. Valerie Lady Charleson. Oh, come on, she's in every paper out.

JIM. I can't read, so I'm not so hot on the names. Faces – fine.

BELLA. Look, I'm matt lacquered, all right? All I know is she's teamed up with Pat Bedford, we haven't had a word from her and she's stayed up London.

JIM. Oh. Was there no message for me?

BELLA. None for you, me or anybody. So we'll see. 'Night.
(*She drives off.*)

The front of the Regent Hotel, early next morning. A small crowd of press is hanging about. BILLY is handing round coffees in a box lid. Parked close by, STELLA is standing by her car looking at an envelope of photos, shots of PAT and MARGARET from last night. BILLY comes over with a coffee for STELLA.

STELLA. Thanks darling. You were wearing that tie on the *Leicester Mercury*.

BILLY. Probably was as well.

STELLA. Yes, these are nice. I'll take these.

BILLY. Oh cheers. Well I'm around all weekend if you want any more.

STELLA. She's cancelled my interview. I thought it was worth a try. Any sign of the sister?

BILLY. Neither of them. She's not taking any calls.

STELLA. Well this is all jolly intriguing. Very nice for little Stella's book.

PAT's *hotel room.* PAT, *fully made up in a very glamorous tracksuit, is doing a workout to her own workout video. The* PAT *on the tape is very flatteringly lit and surrounded by hunky young men. She low-impacts over to the window and sees the press is all still there.*

MARGARET's *room. She dials a number.*

MARGARET. Oh hello Mrs Dench, it's Margaret here. Margaret Mottershead. I tried to get hold of Jim at work but – could you give him a message for me? Can you say I'm sorry about last night, it got too late to phone, and I'm not sure what I have to do here, but I'll come home as soon as I can. I don't think I'll be staying very long, I don't think Pat – well, I miss him loads tell him, and I'll be home soon. Can you pass that on, please? Bye.

The hall of JIM's *house. His mum puts the phone down.* JIM *thunders down the stairs half dressed.*

JIM. Was that Margaret? Is she having a nice time?

MUM. Your Aunty Ivy wanting wool.

JIM turns to go back upstairs.

Your label's out on your vest.

PAT's *room.* MARGARET *pokes her head round the door.*

MARGARET. Hiya! The girl who brought my coffee said you've got more journalists outside than José Carreras – can't be bad.

PAT freezes the frame.

PAT. I'm waiting for Claire, she has my bag, and then I will write you a cheque.

MARGARET. Pardon?

PAT. Just a one-off payment.

MARGARET. No, I'm fine. I got paid yesterday. There was

overtime – I'm fine.

PAT. This won't be a regular thing. I'm already heavily committed charitywise – tropical fish for shut-ins, evening dresses for single mothers –

MARGARET. Sorry, you've lost me.

PAT. So a one-off payment. You sign this, it's just to say we're not related, you're not my sister, you have no claim on Pat Bedford Inc., that's my company.

MARGARET. I'm not signing that.

PAT. What?

MARGARET. I am your sister. You know I am. You recognised me straight away, didn't you.

PAT. Don't sign it till Claire brings the cheque – I'm not trying to be unreasonable.

MARGARET. I don't want the cheque. I haven't got a bank account anyway. I had a surprise last night as well, you know. I didn't want to stay. I could have been on a coach last night having a laugh, could have been at work this morning, not stuck in a room all on my own, having croissants which I don't even like.

PAT. Fine. Go back. But don't go out the front.

MARGARET. Why, 'cos of the journalists?

PAT. They twist things.

MARGARET. There's nothing to twist about me. Met up with a long lost sister, long lost sister didn't want to know, went home.

PAT. There's probably a back way through the kitchens.

MARGARET. Oh well, I'll feel very comfy there then, won't I? It's very me, is kitchens. Oh and here's your pants. Don't worry – I didn't wear them. I washed mine and put them on the towel rail.

PAT. Have them.

MARGARET. No thanks. I don't want anything of yours.

She opens the door and in sails CLAIRE *followed by a camera crew.*

CLAIRE. Morning! This is John, Mike and Sarah. They're doing the *Magic Moments* follow-up film, did I mention it?

PAT. No.

CLAIRE. They'll be following you and Margaret round all day, loads of fun things planned.

The freeze-frame unfreezes.

PAT (*on video*). And give those buns one last squeeze. Relax, you deserve it.

CLAIRE. So, what shall we do? A little bit of filming in here?

PAT. Yes.

CLAIRE. Suppose Pat and Margaret both do the exercise video. Would that be fun?

The lounge of the Regent Hotel. PAT *is giving a press conference, plugging her book and workout video.* STELLA *is very much in the background, whispering to* BILLY. MARGARET *is doing a piece to her own camera crew.*

MARGARET. This is a press conference right, the press are wanting to know about Pat's book, and me, and what I do, all of that. And so far, I'm having a wonderful time! Margaret Mottershead, Regent Hotel, Marylebone, London, the World!

PAT. I have chips, I have chocolate, I pig out, pig out, pig out, but I always have my mango – it's enzymes – all very proven and above hand.

BILLY. Margaret? How have your friends on the motorway taken to all this?

MARGARET. I haven't had a chance to speak to them yet, not even got hold of my boyfriend yet!

BILLY. He's a lav cleaner, isn't he dear? How do you think he'd take to the Californian lifestyle?

MARGARET. He'd probably hate it. I don't know, he can't read, so new places are difficult. I'd like it though, given the chance!

STELLA. Planning to look up family and friends in the North while you're here, Pat?

PAT knows exactly who STELLA is, but keeps cool.

PAT. No, it's a very crammed schedule unfortunately.

STELLA. So, your mother won't be expecting a visit?

PAT. I'm afraid she's no longer with us. But I'm sure she's looking down from somewhere – dear old Vera – sorry, could we leave it there, it's rather upsetting, I miss her now . . .

The conference starts to break up, as PAT seems near to tears.

STELLA. I had a little phone call yesterday.

BILLY. Oh yeah?

STELLA. There's a Vera in an old folks' home in Pat's home town. Fancy a little tripette?

Followed by their crew, PAT and MARGARET visit an exclusive clothes shop where nothing fits MARGARET, and a diner where PAT struggles to make chips.

They finish their little film by the pool in a health club. PAT and MARGARET, both in fluffy robes, are dangling their toes in the water. MARGARET has had her hair and face done.

MARGARET (*shyly*). Well, Pat, LA sounds wonderful.

PAT. Darling, you'll adore it, and with all your gorgeous down-to-earth Northern charm they will adore you! (*She drops her smile and looks past the camera.*) OK?

JOHN. Thank you. That's it, we're done.

PAT. Was the bit about my three houses OK? I would hate to sound ontenstatious. I must get out of this tacky robe. Claire!

The Motorway Services kitchen, the same day. BELLA, *in uniform, surrounded by the usual girls, is talking earnestly to* STELLA, *while* BILLY *snaps away.*

BELLA. The thing is, Stella, we've heard nothing since she got off the coach – I mean how difficult is it to pick up a phone? Apart from her being a mate ho ho, I've got rosters to organise, there's people queuing up to do shift work here – do I hold it open or what?

STELLA. Very difficult for you. Now where can I find Jim?

The health club. PAT, CLAIRE *and the crew are leaving.* MARGARET, *red-faced and hair ruined from the sauna, is fumbling with her bag and purse and anorak at the pay phone. When she sees them leaving she gives up on the call and dashes after them, but is caught on the wrong side of a fish-pond and can't catch up.*

JIM's *living-room. The tea trolley is laden, and* MUM *is in full swing.*

MUM. You see she's not phoned, Stella, no consideration for Jim's feelings. Well it smacks very casual, have an Easter Bakewell.

STELLA. No, I'm full of, what was it – bap?

JIM. To be fair –

MUM. I'm talking, thank you. Because Jim is illiterate – we make no bones over it. They didn't have dyslexia in those days, you sat at the back with raffia.

STELLA. You must feel a little bit sore over this.

JIM. Well, obviously I would like to talk to Margaret on a face-to-face basis.

STELLA. Absolutely. Now, you're a lovely lav cleaner, aren't you? Could we do a few shots with the lavatory? Would there be one indoors, or . . . ?

PAT's *suite.* PAT *lounges on a sofa, on the telephone. A maid is delivering fresh flowers and bottled water.*

PAT. Well Britain is a grubby little third-rate island, darling, but the point is – they love me. And, this terrible firago with the relative from hell has actually been rather a bonus. (*Listens.*) Yes, quite – (*She clicks her fingers at the maid.*) Chicken? *Pollet? Poulenté?* Small portion no skin and nine grapes.

MARGARET *comes in, unnoticed, as the maid scuttles out.*

I mean who needs eight Vietnamese babies when you can have a lumpy old short-order waitress for one week only. Oh no – I'll milk it for all it's worth this week, then I'll go home and she can take a flying – yes quite – at a deep-fat fryer! Oh, she's horrendous – the perm, the funny voice – I mean it's real Tracey Ullman time. (*She sees* MARGARET.) Yes? I'm talking.

MARGARET *goes through to her room.*

OK darling, and tell them at the meeting Valerie Lady Charleson is red hot in England, she wants some bloody good story-lines next season. *Ciao.*

Early Sunday morning. A paper-girl shoves papers into the letterbox of JIM's *house. In the kitchen,* JIM *is having his breakfast. His* MUM *stabs a finger at the Sunday paper.*

MUM. You'll recognise that word, 'Margaret'.

JIM. Yes.

MUM. 'It's bye bye Motorway, hello LA, she laughed. There is nothing and no one to keep me here, meeting up with Pat again has been a real godsend.'

BELLA's *hall.* BELLA, *in rather unglamorous nightwear, has just picked up the paper.*

BELLA (*shouting*). 'Meeting Pat again has been a godsend. The job is rubbish, it's hey hey LA for me.'

Sunday morning, the Kirkby Arms Hotel restaurant, Lancashire. STELLA, BILLY *and a* STRINGER *from the local paper sit over breakfast with the nationals.*

STELLA. That's made a nice little column, you see. Bolshy Bella and Jilted Jim. 'Too slow for fast food.'

STRINGER. Did she actually say that?

STELLA. Snap on dear. Now – Pat Bedford. What have you got for me?

STRINGER. Well a lot of the old files were fire-damaged. I've got her old address, school, few bits and bobs. The address of the mother's nursing home is in there.

STELLA. Oh well, thanks darling. Oh, and did you dig out any local scandals?

BILLY. Eh?

STELLA. Well if we have to be in the bloody North darling, I might as well get a column or two out of it.

BILLY. Terrible marmalade.

STRINGER. Well, there's the man who kept the dogs in the dark with no –

STELLA. No dogs. Done dogs to death.

STRINGER. There's the baby boom faulty condom thing.

STELLA. Mm.

STRINGER. This Spanish Villa thing's a big thing here. A local couple built an apartment complex over a chemical dump – no one can get their money back, little old couples have lost their life savings.

STELLA. Well, give me the files, I'll have a look through. (*She slaps some money on the table.*) Give me a receipt for that, could you. Come on Bill, let's get to the old folks' home before they all do. Fancy tipping off two papers -- you can't trust anybody.

PAT's *bathroom, Sunday morning.* PAT, *admiring herself in the papers, sees one photo she's not so keen on and goes to check her neck in the mirror.* MARGARET *comes in in her anorak.*

MARGARET. I'm just going for a walk or something. We're not doing anything till this afternoon are we?

PAT. No. Would you have your neck done if you were me?

MARGARET. If I were you I'd have a personality transplant.

PAT. You see I do this every day. (*She pulls up her bottom lip.*) And I think that does actually stop it sagging. Be too late for you.

MARGARET. Are we in the papers?

PAT. Every single one. Look -- my legs on this one are just gorgeous.

MARGARET. Jim gets this paper. Well his mum reads it to him. What's this -- I never said the job was rubbish. They've made half of this up. (*She snatches up another paper.*) That's Bella, they've been talking to Bella.

BELLA's *hall.* BELLA *is still riveted by the papers.*

BELLA. 'I have no reason to keep the job open. Margaret is no loss, quite frankly, she is too slow for fast food.' I never said that. They've picked that bit out in big letters.

JIM's *kitchen.*

MUM. These bigger letters here say 'Too slow for fast food'.

JIM. Now that's not fair.

MUM. Shall I read you what it says about you again?

JIM. No.

MUM. 'Lavatory attendant, Jim, who has learning difficulties' – that's nice –

JIM. Is there a phone number?

MUM. In the paper? For Pat Bedford? She'd be inundated with trouser fumblers. Remember Mrs Anglesey, and the post office window? She was only trying to sell a divan.

JIM. Does it say where they're staying?

MUM. The Regent Hotel. Marylebone Road.

JIM. What road?

MUM. Marylebone. Mary-le-bone.

JIM. Marylebone.

MUM. Where are you off to?

JIM. There. Marylebone Road. You've got Ivy coming. I'll be back in time to open the corned beef. Please Mum, all right?

PAT's *suite*. MARGARET *collects her bag and checks her pockets.*

MARGARET. You see I don't think I've even got Bella's number. Anyway, I'm hopeless on the phone. Where is it the coaches go from, is it Victoria? You wouldn't know.

PAT (*still admiring her newspaper photos*). What?

MARGARET. I'll go straight to the coach station. I'll go to Jim's first, no, Bella's first. You see they don't have to give you notice now, we're all on those funny shift contracts.

PAT. But it's the little telly thing this afternoon.

MARGARET. Well I can't do it.

PAT. It's television.

MARGARET. Well this is my job. I have a life too you know. I might be just a waitress with a perm and a funny voice, but I can remember when you were a waitress with the same voice and you were pretty pleased with yourself to be one.

PAT. Look, I'll call Claire. She can call Jim, is it, and Bella. She'll smooth the whole thing over.

MARGARET. Oh don't be so flipping thick. What's Claire got to do with Bella – just 'cos you can't exist without Claire; even the Queen carries her own handbag you know.

PAT. Just stay a couple more days. It's *Hello!* magazine on Monday. Hampstead Heath remember? The eight-page spread and the leopard-skin leggings? Go on.

MARGARET. I thought you were going to say 'please' then. That'd be worth a front page picture.

PAT. Please.

MARGARET. Oh come on. I might be daft but I'm not stupid. You had me halfway out through the kitchens yesterday morning, a film crew come on the doorstep and suddenly I'm our delicious Margaret with my lovely Northern charm.

PAT. Well, that's show business. Suit yourself. I can have a virus, fly back early.

MARGARET. Right. No harm done then.

PAT. Want a memento of your fifteen minutes of fame? An Andy Warhol quote, you won't have heard of him, he wasn't very big in catering.

She folds up a paper to give MARGARET *and suddenly freezes.*

MARGARET. What's the matter?

PAT *points to a paragraph.*

What?

PAT. Vera. Little paragraph about Vera.

MARGARET. What?

PAT. That she's in a nursing home, up there.

MARGARET. I never thought she was dead.

PAT. No, but they'll find her.

MARGARET. Who?

PAT. Any of them! Stella Kincaid. She was there yesterday. She's trying to get something on me, I'm sure.

MARGARET. She's only an old woman, Vera – where's the harm?

PAT. They'd see her. They'd see her and then see me. They'd think I was like her. I hate her. I can't let her do it to me twice.

MARGARET. What?

PAT. I can't let her ruin it all, make everything dirty again. I'm not that person now. She doesn't know me.

MARGARET. She might not even want to talk to them.

PAT. Oh come on. They pay thousands. Don't you think she'd talk? The woman who did it standing up for ten Bensons.

MARGARET. And lying down for twenty.

PAT. It would finish me. Photo this size – some stinking old biddy with a crocheted blanket watching the test card. 'Glamor Star's Mother in Council Home Hell.' And that's before they've heard her side of the story. I'll have to find her. I'll have to find her before they do.

MARGARET. And what, ask her not to say anything?

PAT. Pay her not to say anything. When did she ever do anything for nothing? Not for me. Do you remember how she was?

MARGARET. I remember all of it.

PAT. I'll call Claire. No, we can't go crawling around in that huge limo, not round there. Will you come with me?

MARGARET. God, I don't want to see her.

PAT. I don't know which nursing home. I don't know her surname. People know me, I can't go round asking questions.

MARGARET. Wear a wig. Take Claire.

PAT. This is all private stuff. This is horrible, secret, stuffed away – this is the stuff in the back of the wardrobe. I daren't go on my own.

MARGARET. Is this all real or what?

PAT. Yes. Please. And once we've choked her off, I'll get you to Bella's and Jim's – and I'll explain how it is to them. Really, I can sort it out for you.

MARGARET. All right.

PAT. I mean we are sisters.

MARGARET. We're two middle-aged women in a mess, you mean.

The hotel foyer. PAT, *in a wig and what she would consider casual clothes, is on the phone.*

PAT. I don't know whether it's worth waiting for Claire anyway. By the time she's fannied about with her nipple shells and her maternity knickers – Claire? Yes, cancel the TV, I don't know about tomorrow yet – Look – we'll go now – you follow us up with the bags and meet us – shut up – What's the biggest hotel?

MARGARET. Kirkby Arms, I suppose.

PAT. Meet us in the Kirkby Arms this evening. Don't book me in, I'll be incognito. The Kirkby Arms – I used to drink port and lemon in there.

PORTER. The car's outside, Miss Bedford. The keys are in.

MARGARET. What's the matter?

PAT. Stella went North yesterday – come on!

Outside the hotel. They climb into a small saloon.

PAT. I don't believe this! Gears! It's not an automatic. This bloody country! Good Christ, is it not hard enough pointing a car in the right direction without fiddling with a great big stiff knob at the same time. Can you drive one of these?

MARGARET. Not exactly.

STELLA *and* BILLY *go down the front steps of the old folks' home.*

BILLY. Well, there we go. Home?

STELLA. Oh no darling. I've got lots of little leads in my folder. I haven't nearly finished with black pudding country yet.

The M6 motorway. JIM's car whizzes along. A green-lettered strip over the windscreen says 'JIM' and 'MARGARET'. As his car passes the Services, PAT's car jerks and stutters and pulls in on the opposite side.

Motorway Services. PAT waits by the Ladies with a couple of drinks and a sandwich. She's reading the labels as MARGARET joins her. They head back for the car, passing a young family all screaming and throwing food about.

PAT. They should video that if they want people to use condoms.

MARGARET. Perhaps they're tired from travelling.

PAT's *car. They drive a little way along the motorway in silence.*

MARGARET. I was having a baby once. It never went the full – they probably have more equipment now. Funny year. Gary died in the June, and then I lost her in the, well, it was about now.

PAT. Were you married then?

MARGARET. Yeah. He had an accident at work. I was going to get compensation, there was some reason why I didn't.

PAT. I don't know why people have children.

MARGARET. Do you not have any?

PAT. No. And my friends don't have any. And my dogs don't have any. All very civilised.

STELLA and BILLY *doorstep on* PAT's *old estate. They photograph her school, talk to her old neighbours.*

The front of the Regent Hotel. As the PORTER *loads the bags into* CLAIRE's *car,* JIM *pulls up and parks happily under the* ABSOLUTELY NO PARKING *sign. He dashes in.*

PORTER. Oi! Can't you read?

JIM. No.

The PORTER's *desk.*

PORTER. Miss Bedford's car is on the forecourt, madam, the driver's waiting, the bags are in.

CLAIRE. Oh good-oh. I'll be two ticks – I absolutely have to spend a penny. Pregnant!

PAT's *old house. It is little changed from 1958, but the windows are boarded up.* STELLA *stands outside with the old busybody from next door, who holds a photo album.*

BUSYBODY. Pregnant at fifteen. Mind you, with a mother like that.

STELLA. So you knew Vera.

BUSYBODY. Everybody knew Vera. Curtains drawn in the afternoon and she wasn't watching Wimbledon. Hang on.

STELLA. Really.

BUSYBODY. We were surprised Pat didn't fall pregnant sooner. I thought – our John took this – that's Vera – now when was that – when did 'Boom Bang-a-Bang' win the Eurovision Song Contest?

STELLA. Could I borrow this? What did Pat have, an abortion?

BUSYBODY. Ooh no, you couldn't get abortions round here then. We didn't get muesli till last year.

The PORTER's *desk.* JIM *stands rather lost by the desk.* CLAIRE *stops on her way out.*

CLAIRE (*speaking to the receptionist*). Could you pass that on to the switchboard, that's the number, and that's any messages for Miss Bedford, me or Miss Mottershead. Thank you.

JIM. Sorry, did you say Mottershead?

CLAIRE. Yes.

JIM. You're not like a friend of Margaret's are you?

CLAIRE. Well I'm working for Miss Bedford while she's over here.

JIM. I've just like driven down to see Margaret.

CLAIRE. Oh, are you Jim? Oh how ghastly. They've gone north. They went north this morning. You've just come down and they've gone up! Oh what a calamity, what can I do?

JIM. Not to worry, I'll drive back up and track her down.

CLAIRE. Oh, what a bind! Look, how can I help? I think Margaret's so gorgeous . . .

A derelict maternity home on the main road. STELLA *turns over the original sign, lying in the weeds:* SORRENTO MATERNITY HOME, PROP: MRS K. MATHER.

STELLA. Must have been grim, mustn't it?

BILLY. What now?

STELLA. The Red Lion? Do you have to fiddle with your testicles the entire time?

JIM's car. CLAIRE settles herself in as he drives through London.

CLAIRE. No, it's much cosier this way isn't it? I can keep you company, read the road signs, we can have a jolly good old chin-wag.

JIM. Fair enough.

CLAIRE. Though I must warn you, since week seventeen, I've had the most ghastly wind. Real stinkers.

JIM nods gamely, bright red.

The main road. PAT's car passes the maternity home. The car stops.

MARGARET. That's not it.

PAT gets out.

That was the unmarried mothers' home – do you remember? We used to see them mopping the front steps.

PAT doesn't answer as she gets out of the car and looks at the derelict building. We hear 'Big Spender' as played on a transistor radio, the voices of young girls laughing and singing.

The hall of the old folks' home. A HELPER approaches as PAT and MARGARET hover. PAT keeps her face away.

PAT. You ask.

MARGARET. You ask.

PAT. I'm the celebrity – you ask.

HELPER. Yeah?

MARGARET. Hello! Do you have a Vera?

HELPER. The boiler?

MARGARET. No, an old lady.

HELPER. Oh, Vera! Yeah. I'll show you. (*She leads the way.*)
She never sees nobody normally, you're the second lot today.

PAT winces.

She's down there. In Gladioli. Just past Hyacinth. (*She turns
away.*) John! Go and sniff that mince for me!

PAT and MARGARET go along the corridor slowly.

PAT. I can't go in.

*MARGARET goes on ahead. She knocks on the door of a two-
bedded room. One OLD LADY sits by the door, another stares out
of the window.*

MARGARET. I'm looking for Vera.

The one seated nods at the other.

OLD LADY. You won't get any sense out of her.

MARGARET. Mum? It's Margaret, Mum.

The second old lady, VERA, turns from the window.

VERA. I'm not your mum. My girl's Julie Andrews. Beautiful
Julie. 'Feed the birds, tuppence a bag.'

*MARGARET shakes her head at PAT who has come as far as
the doorway.*

MARGARET. It's not her.

They walk slowly away from the room.

PAT. I was dreading seeing her face. I have dreams even now,
I've borrowed her blouse, and she's shouting – and – I was so
scared then.

MARGARET. Even before she turned round I was thinking –
it's not her. It just wasn't like Vera.

PAT. Where is she then really? I've got to find her. She can't
take it all away from me again.

HELPER. Did you get any sense out of her? She's semi-barking most of the time. She were Pat Bedford's mother all last week – that one even got in the papers!

JIM's car. He has relaxed a little and is quite chatty.

JIM. I'd not really come across this PA job before.

CLAIRE. Well a lot of it's very basic in this case. Get Pat to the right place, at the right time with the right bag. Our turn-off next.

JIM. But she's driven up with it herself today. The luggage.

CLAIRE. It's in the limo. I've left them all behind. Oh Crikey Moses.

A petrol station. The forecourt is stacked with logs, plastic cartons and twelve-pound shell suits. MARGARET is filling the car with petrol penny by penny, while PAT watches and sips a soft drink.

PAT. Come on.

MARGARET. I haven't got much money left you know.

PAT. As soon as I get my bag off Claire –

She sees BILLY strolling back to the car with a lolly. STELLA is in the car with the door open, scanning her files. PAT drags MARGARET out of the way, and they back up behind a car where a girl has all the doors open, shaking her mats. She fiddles with a token, trying to get it in the jet-wash.

STELLA. Billy – where's that photo album?

BILLY. We back on Vera?

STELLA. No, this is the Spanish Villa hoo-ha. You drive, I've just seen the most . . .

BILLY drives away. The girl succeeds with the token, the jet-wash starts suddenly and drenches PAT completely.

PAT. I'd like to thank everybody for making this possible. Thank you. Thank you.

JIM's living-room. CLAIRE is coming to the end of a sobbing fit, MUM is in attendance with damp cloths and cups of tea. JIM stands by rather helplessly.

CLAIRE. I'm so sorry, I can't believe I've been so stupid, it's my hormones you see, my memory's completely – I don't know what I'm going to do – I have to get Pat's things to the Kirkby Arms this evening.

JIM. The car you were going to come in, could you not ask it to come up with the bags like?

CLAIRE. Inspiration! Genius! Of course, I'll phone the hotel. Could I wait here for them, would you mind?

MUM *offers a damp cloth.*

CLAIRE. Oh thank you. Mm what a lovely smell. Is it lavender?

MUM. It's actually a urinal disinfectant, Jim brings it from work.

CLAIRE. Oh dear, I never cried before I was pregnant, it must be the hormones.

MUM. Oh it will be. I knew a woman that only ate luncheon meat the whole nine months.

CLAIRE. Was the baby all right?

MUM. It was all right then. It ended up selling insurance in Chorlton. So there's no saying, is there.

The very neat garden of a small semi. MR LLOYD stands in his garden, a FOR SALE/REPOSSESSION *board up. He's been clipping the hedge. STELLA and BILLY are standing on the pavement on the other side of the hedge.*

MR LLOYD. We'd always liked Spain, and these villas came up, and we thought one for us, one to rent out – we've lost everything basically. My wife can't go out, I don't think she'll recover. Worked all my life, we both have. And there seems to be no redress at all – I've been round their house, to reason with them – it's all dogs and gates, you've no chance. It's not the money so much as what it's done to Mrs Lloyd.

PAT's old estate. Grey and empty, there's nobody about. PAT, somehow managing to look OK in a shell suit, is shouting at MARGARET.

PAT. Is that really all the cash you've got on you?

MARGARET. I've bought everything today. And I need most of that for rent.

PAT. Rent?

MARGARET. I rent a bedsitter.

PAT. Oh. I'd imagined a little terrace, or a semi.

MARGARET. Oh had you. It's a pity I live in real life and not your imagination.

PAT (*stopping*). Oh bloody hell.

MARGARET. What?

PAT. That bench. And the bus shelter. I can't believe it's just stayed like this all this time. (*She shakes her head to clear the memory.*) It's still dusty. It was always so dusty, and crisp bags blowing about –

They turn the corner into their old street. They stare at the boarded-up house. PAT *looks up at the bathroom windows. She hears:*

VOICE OF VERA. I'm wetting my bloody pants here!

VOICE OF YOUNG PAT. Oh, sorry, I didn't think you wore any!

PAT. You shove it all away, move on, grow up, cut your hair, and it's all there waiting, isn't it, waiting to be dealt with.

MARGARET. I don't really know what you mean.

PAT. Look – go and get a taxi, find Bella – at least put that bit of it right. I'll get the cash biked over to you as soon as I can.

MARGARET. Biked?

PAT. You go. This is my stuff. We've all got our nasty old wardrobes, haven't we? Where is she? She couldn't have got away, people don't.

MARGARET. You did.

PAT. Everybody knows me. Why has she never tried to find me?

MARGARET. She can't have wanted to. She can't have wanted to find either of us. (*She hears:*)

VOICE OF VERA. I don't know what you're howling for – you never got on with her when she was here. Now go and post that bloody pools coupon.

VOICE OF YOUNG MARGARET. I did! I did get on with her! She'll come back for me anyway, she wouldn't leave me here with you.

VOICE OF VERA. Are you cheeking me?

The next-door BUSYBODY *looms up behind them.*

BUSYBODY. Do you recognise me? Next door! We always said you'd go far. *Lakeland Vet* – we loved that.

Another street on the same estate. PAT *and* MARGARET *walk along, checking the numbers.*

MARGARET. I just don't remember this family at all.

PAT. Well the mother was just like our mother, only vertical, but the daughter was really glamorous, had a little black shiny mac, really belted in, really high heels – big beehive, I used to hang over the gate, I just wanted to be her. Lorraine!

MARGARET. This is it.

JIM's *house.* CLAIRE *and* MUM *are having yet more cups of tea.*

CLAIRE. Are you sure this is all right, waiting here for the bags? I thought it was safer.

MUM. No, that's fine. (*Lowering her voice.*) Anyway, I like Jim to be exposed to different types of women. Margaret's all very well in her way, but she's not upwardly mobile. I have a lovely friend who would take him on pronto, she's very high up in gum hygiene. A bit of a depressive but as I say to Jim, you don't want to be enjoying yourself all the time.

CLAIRE. Ooh.

MUM. Kicking? Jim was the same, I had his foot in my kidneys from the July. In the event, he was all placenta and he had to wear a golliwog's jumper. He did. We pulled him through but that was it for me. I said to my husband, twin beds and a budgie.

The closed gates of a large modern house. STELLA *stands with* BILLY *and speaks into the entryphone.*

STELLA. Mrs McIntyre? Could you let me in, please? My name's Stella Kincaid, you may have read my column, and I've got five thousand pounds in cash in my handbag.

A small and very untidy living-room. LORRAINE, *an unhappy-looking woman of about fifty, comes into the room where* PAT *and* MARGARET *are waiting in company with three silent adolescents sprawled about. The room is dirty and cluttered.*

LORRAINE. My mum says the last she heard Vera was cleaning at the Red Lion in town.

PAT. Thanks.

MARGARET. We tried there. It's all new people now.

LORRAINE. Done well for yourself.

PAT. Well, you know, right place at the right time.

LORRAINE. Is that it? Must have been in wrong place, me.

PAT. Was it your sister who used to come past our gate on the way to work? Lorraine?

LORRAINE. That were me. Did you not recognise me?

OLD MOTHER (*from upstairs*). Lorraine! Hitch me up!

LORRAINE (*to her mother*). Hang on! (*To* PAT *and* MARGARET.) See yourselves out. You look older off, did you know?

The reception desk of the Kirkby Arms. PAT *and* MARGARET *are at the desk, trying to check in. Trainee receptionist* EMMA-LOUISE, *nineteen, is on the computer. There is a 'do' on and drunk women in pink cocktail dresses are weaving in and out of the Ladies.*

PAT. Let's start again. Has a Claire Wellesley checked in or left a message?

EMMA-LOUISE. No.

PAT. Right. I would like a suite for me and a single for Miss Wellesley.

EMMA-LOUISE. We don't have suites.

MARGARET. They're bad for your teeth.

EMMA-LOUISE. I can do you a large non-smoking ladies' with operational balcony.

PAT. Ladies'?

EMMA-LOUISE. It's pink with cotton-wool balls and scatter cushions.

PAT. Whatever.

EMMA-LOUISE. Could I trouble you for two forms of ID?

PAT. My face is my ID.

EMMA-LOUISE. I'm afraid we don't accept faces.

PAT. My cards are coming with Miss Wellesley.

EMMA-LOUISE. I'm fully comprehensive re that, it's just that with you having no cash or no credit cards, and given that we in the leisure industry have had our fingers fairly badly burned on this one.

PAT. I am Patricia Bedford.

EMMA-LOUISE. Yes, but notwithstanding, I do have to adhere to the procedure. This is laid down, that we adhere to the procedure.

PAT. Fetch the manager.

    EMMA-LOUISE *escapes behind the two-way mirror.*

    I don't believe this! ID! We were both plastered all over the Sunday papers this morning.

    Two middle-aged LADIES *weave past.*

FIRST LADY. I know how you feel, love.

SECOND LADY. Look – it's her from *Glamor* – Valerie –

FIRST LADY. Valerie Lady Charleson. You were in a right quandary last week, weren't you?

SECOND LADY. Give up on the publishing –

FIRST LADY. She didn't know whether to expand on the publishing side –

SECOND LADY. Or give it all up.

FIRST LADY. Give it all up.

SECOND LADY. Because Brent loves her.

FIRST LADY. He does, he does love you.

    MR SCRUTON, *the seventeen-year-old hotel manager, stands behind the desk.*

SECOND LADY. Yeah, but he's never told her – he's only told Malcolm Halliday in the locker-room.

FIRST LADY. That's why she can't decide. (*In Valerie's voice.*) 'Don't hassle me, Brent! *Glamor* magazine needs me, and right at this moment in time – I just – don't – know!'

    The two women burst into the Glamor *theme tune and stroll off back to their 'do', arms linked.*

PAT. You see? I don't need cash, I don't need ID. Those are my ID – the great marvellous warm caring British public!

MR SCRUTON. As Emma-Louise may have mentioned, we do have to adhere to a procedure.

PAT. I don't care if you have to adhere to a baboon's bumhole. In fact compared with this rancid pile of olde-worlde knick-knacks a primate's backside begins to look like the epitome of gracious living.

MARGARET. Could we not wait till our friend arrives with Pat's handbag?

MR SCRUTON. While I have no objection to you sitting in the public areas, madam, I'm afraid your companion fails to meet the requirements of our dress code.

PAT. What?

MR SCRUTON *points to a printed card on the desk:* MANAGEMENT REGRETS NO HEAVY WORK CLOTHES NO DENIMS NO SHELL SUITS. *As* PAT *stares at the notice,* STELLA *and* BILLY *in a cosy corner crack open the champagne.*

PAT's *car heads towards a modern estate.*

MARGARET. She's got this guest room and a shower, and those curtains, what are they, whooshed, ruched! She did say, any time . . .

BELLA's *house. She opens the door and stares at* MARGARET *and* PAT.

MARGARET. Bella. Did you read the papers this morning?

BELLA. Yes I did. We all did. Very interesting to hear you've no friends and the job's rubbish. So I didn't bother putting you on next week's roster.

MARGARET. The thing is, they make it up, virtually.

BELLA. Do they, virtually? So you're not her sister and you're not off to Cali-Bloody-Fornia.

MARGARET. I didn't say it. I came round to tell you that, and to just say is there any way Pat could have a bed for the night?

BELLA. Not interested, sorry. I pity you, frankly, I had you down as genuine. I organised that coach trip, I made sure you were on that coach – you couldn't even be fagged to find me to come and say bye-bye.

PAT. Look – hang on –

BELLA. Could you take your hand off my paintwork please. I'm not impressed with celebrities actually. From what I read they're thinking of taking off that *Glamor* anyway – so you'll be just another ex-has-been. Frankly I'm amazed your bosses let you dress like that. I don't know what you paid for that in LA, but round here they're going for ten ninety-nine.

She shuts the door. They turn away.

PAT. Bloody cheek. It was twelve quid.

JIM's house. CLAIRE, on her ninth cup of tea, is flagging rather in the gloomy company of MUM.

MUM. Fibroids? Like baked potatoes.

JIM comes in cheerfully.

JIM. He's got all the bags no problem. So whenever you're ready he'll take you round to the hotel.

CLAIRE. Oh that's marvellous. I'll just nip to the loo, then you must let me reimburse you for the tea.

JIM. Not to worry.

MUM. Don't stop her. With her bladder, this has cost me three pounds in Harpic alone.

JIM. I'll see she gets to the hotel all right, shall I?

MUM. Is that Margaret going to be there? Is that the scheme?

Well I would think on hard and sharp before I got more convoluted with her, bluntly. She's playing you for a giddy kipper; she'll be laughing about you now with that sister.

JIM. If she's there I want to talk to her.

MUM. Well the chain goes on at the usual time.

PAT's car pulls up outside a corner shop. MARGARET gets out and unlocks a small side door.

MARGARET's bedsit. MARGARET unlocks the door and goes straight to the cooker and lights all four jets. She's joined by PAT, who looks round the small room, furnished with nasty old pieces but brightened up with MARGARET's ornaments and mug-trees, framed tea towels, etc.

MARGARET (*lighting the fire*). It'll warm up in a minute. (*She brings in a pint of milk from the window-sill and sniffs it.*)

PAT. Don't you have a fridge?

MARGARET. There is a fridge but I wouldn't leave anything in it. It's off, sorry. Got some powdered.

PAT. What I could really do with is some food.

MARGARET. I don't think I've got much in. Jim usually takes me Saturday, do a big shop. Well, he did.

PAT. That's OK. Look – shall I cook you my absolute favourite thing? It's really simple – you just need virgin olive oil, any pasta, beef tomatoes, fresh basil we can manage without – dried herbs then, and an avocado.

MARGARET opens the door of her food cupboard and takes out, one by one, a 'Variety'-size packet of Special K, a small tin of spaghetti, a tin of powdered milk and a jar of pickle.

MARGARET. That's what I've got. Does that count as pasta – tinned spaghetti? I don't have the things you have. I don't have three houses and a swimming-pool and an open-top –

PAT. Mercedes.

MARGARET. This is me. This is where I live, and it's not nice – and I know I spent all yesterday saying I wasn't jealous and I was just glad to see you and I was happy living the way I do – well I'm not. I don't want to be like this – I want what you've got!

PAT. Then work for it! You've no idea what I had to do to get where I am now – do something!

MARGARET. What can I do? I can't do anything. I wanted a husband and a house and a baby, well I told you what – you could do something – I couldn't do anything. I'm not clever, I couldn't be a manageress. I don't know how to earn any more money – other people have husbands, I can't buy a house, I'd have loved a little house – not a room where they come in when you're not here and look in your things – you had something.

PAT. Yes I did –

MARGARET. Yes, well you should have helped me!

PAT. What?

MARGARET. Why did you leave me?

There's a thumping on the wall. They look at each other.

PAT. That isn't what happened.

MARGARET. It is what happened. You went. I was eleven. She got done again.

PAT. Suspended sentence.

MARGARET. No – the real thing. It wasn't for long but – she never really got it together after that – I was just sort of fostered about. It wasn't that bad. I just used to think you might turn up. You know, sports car, trouser suit, just kid rubbish.

The doorbell rings.

My bell never rings.

She leaves the room. PAT looks around. On the bed is an extremely well-worn cuddly lion nightdress case, all bald. PAT touches it.

MARGARET opens the street door, to see JIM on the doorstep with PAT's handbag. The limo is parked nearby.

MARGARET. Where did you get this?

JIM. Well, it's from Claire. Could you give it to Pat?

MARGARET. How do you know Pat, I mean Claire?

JIM. I gave her a lift from London. I'd gone to see you, only you'd already come here.

MARGARET. Well hello.

JIM. Hello.

MARGARET. I did phone, loads of times.

They go to kiss.

That bloody cardigan.

JIM. This? What's up with it?

MARGARET. Oh nothing. I'm just sick of seeing it. Typical this isn't it. Missed you like mad since Friday, done a million exciting things, just wanted to come back and see you, and now –

JIM. What, you're wishing you hadn't?

MARGARET. Oh I don't know. It's not as if Pat was happy either, and she's got everything. It was just nice to feel something was happening. You and me, nothing's happening.

JIM. I'm not with you.

MARGARET. It's been a funny day, that's all. Look – come in and meet Pat – I feel like I've been wrong-footed all weekend 'cos she doesn't know anything about me and what I've got. I'm just feeling funny tonight – come in for a bit, eh?

JIM. Well, it's just that –

MARGARET. What?

JIM. Well, Mum'll be putting the chain on quite soon.

MARGARET. Phone her! Shove the door in! How long can we piddle along like this – she can't open her sardines, she can't unscrew her hot-water bottle – I want something. I want you to come in and meet my sister – my family – I've never asked you for anything – money, a baby – we should be able to ask each other for things – I want us to be together, but I can't always be accommodating everybody. Jim!

JIM. I'll go and phone Auntie Ivy –

MARGARET. Oh I'm tired of this. I knew she chose your underpants and took the peel out of your marmalade, but – I've had enough. That's us done – she's done it – I give in.

She slams the door on a puzzled JIM.

MARGARET'*s bedsit.* PAT *gives* MARGARET *a mug of tea.*

MARGARET. Ta. Claire's at the hotel. That was Jim with your handbag for some reason, and we've just had a row and I've finished with him. You found the powdered milk then.

The bar of the Kirkby Arms. JIM *is glooming over a drink with* CLAIRE.

JIM. You see, she's only thinking of me, my mother.

CLAIRE. No that's not true.

JIM. Eh?

CLAIRE. No, she's thinking of herself, which is fine and jolly sensible, as long as you do too. (*She stands up.*) What have I had? One orange juice – mad!

CLAIRE *goes off to the loo and* STELLA *sees her go.*

STELLA. Pat's not going to track down the old mum is she? I mean we had a real stroke of luck there, we were way off beam. No, we have to get Pat to Vera's.

BILLY. Well, that's going to be the photo, isn't it?

STELLA *scribbles on a piece of paper and waves at* JIM.

STELLA. Jim! Could you see Pat gets this?

JIM. Pardon?

STELLA. Just a note from a fan, no need to mention me. Night night.

MARGARET'*s bedsit.*

MARGARET. Pat?

PAT. Mm?

MARGARET. Why didn't you take me with you? I were right tall, I could have passed for fourteen.

PAT. Did she say I'd run away? She chucked me out. I was pregnant.

MARGARET. Did you have it?

PAT. Yes I did. It took bloody hours. No painkillers, just those awful women coming in and saying 'It'll get worse before it gets better, Pat Mottershead!' Never again.

MARGARET. They have epidurals now.

PAT. They have stairlifts but I don't want one of them either.

MARGARET. You could have come back after.

PAT. I did. Hobbled back straight after – all soggy bra and sanitary towels – no one there. She was inside I suppose. You and me couldn't have lived together. Ten and fifteen? There was a girl at the home – we hitched down to London, she knew a photographer, I did a bit of modelling. They laugh at Swinging London now but it was heaven on earth to me.

MARGARET. Whose was it? The baby.

PAT. Do you remember my Saturday job in that café? The

Swiss Cottage? Run by the only homosexual in north-east
Lancashire? It was the boy who delivered the Pepsis I got
pregnant with. We only did it once. He had a condom but he
couldn't get it on. He thought that bit at the end had to go
on as well. Come on, I'm buying you dinner.

MARGARET. Where?

PAT. Mind your own business, Margaret Mottershead. Turn the
fire off then, gas isn't cheap you know.

A dark side-street, full of closed businesses. PAT *is leading*
MARGARET *towards the one lighted window – the Swiss Cottage
Café. They go in.*

*The décor is a mixture of fifties coffee bar, all-night truck stop and
'Swiss' tea-shop. The customers are a strange mixture of obviously gay
couples, deaf couples, art students and a few hard-faced blokes. Behind
the counter is* PETE, *elegant, sixtyish, blue rinse and a cravat – the
old-style queen.* PAT *approaches the counter.*

PETE. Don't tell me. A bacon sandwich, a doughnut and a
Pepsi float.

PAT (*in original accent*). I'll pay you back Saturday.

They laugh and hug each other.

PETE. What can I get you?

PAT. A thirty-two.

PETE. With the double fried bread?

PAT. Of course. Margaret, phone Claire, she shouldn't miss out
on this.

MARGARET. You phone her, I'm choosing.

PAT. Cheeky.

The Swiss Cottage, a little later. CLAIRE, MARGARET *and* PAT
are all very jolly over a bottle of wine. PETE *brings over the plates.*

PETE. There's your thirty-two, Patricia. Egg, chips and peas, Margaret.

PAT. That's Claire's – our Margaret doesn't like peas.

CLAIRE. Yummee! This is such a treat, everybody. Chin chin.

PAT. None of it looks any different. You don't look any different.

PETE. I'm sixty-seven.

PAT. You're never.

PETE. Selling up. Soon as I can find a buyer. Quit while you can still smack the ketchup, that's my feeling.

MARGARET. It's lovely. I'm very impressed with these chips.

PAT. Margaret's in chips. Pete – you don't know where my mother ended up, do you? Our mother.

PETE. The terrible Vera. Well we used to see her hanging round the Red Lion, but that's twenty years ago.

PAT. We've asked at the Red Lion.

PETE. Now, who would know?

CLAIRE. Aargh!

PETE. Oh my God, boiling water somebody!

CLAIRE. The note!

PAT *reads* STELLA's *note.*

The gates of the modern house, as before. The next morning.

PAT. This can't be right.

MARGARET. The note only said she'd be here this morning, it didn't say she lived here. She might be the cleaner.

PAT. She might run a mobile blow-job service. (*Pause.*) I don't want to see her.

MARGARET. You've got to.

PAT. This is making me sick.

MARGARET. She'll just be a little old lady. Come on, let's get it over with. It's this one.

They walk into the house. Odd pieces of furniture are on the lawn and piled up in the hall. PAT and MARGARET go up the stairs and stop in the bedroom doorway. The room is in chaos, clothes and shoes everywhere. There is a noise from the bathroom. PAT and MARGARET move over to the doorway. A figure with its back to them is packing toiletries into a supermarket trolley bag. She turns and stares at them with no expression, then carries on packing.

VERA. Bit late for Mother's Day, aren't you?

PAT. Actually, we were hoping to visit your grave but we're a bit early.

VERA. I suppose it were too good to last, you had to track me down eventually. You want to get your neck done – Pat – you can be in and out in two days.

PAT. Recognise Margaret?

VERA. Can't miss her. What do you do?

MARGARET. I work on the motorway – in the cafeteria.

VERA. Your father wasn't much cop at anything either. (*She goes into the bedroom and starts holding clothes up against herself.*)

PAT. Have the press been here?

VERA. About the villas? They're in my name but I've never seen a penny.

PAT. No – what have you been saying about me?

VERA. Nothing. I don't know anything about you. I know you're on the telly, but we only watch the dog trials. Tricky colour, lime green.

PAT *and* MARGARET *sit down on the bed.*

PAT. I didn't realise prostitution was so lucrative.

VERA. I don't think it is. I think you have to enjoy it to earn big money. I didn't mind the sex but I was never very good at talking to them.

PAT. So where did all this come from?

VERA. Pools.

PAT. Not the bloody pools!

The atmosphere starts to loosen. VERA *looks through her dressing-table drawers.*

VERA. That was the start. Won the bloody pools. Ticked no publicity, Caribbean cruise, met my Robert – he couldn't believe it – own teeth, a few bob and I could do shorthand.

PAT. Lovely.

VERA (*moving out on to the landing*). He's skipped off now, of course. Rat. What do you want, I'm busy. If your paw's out wanting money, forget it, it's tied up and you're way down the queue.

The removal men pass her and go into another bedroom.

PAT. You've got a nerve.

VERA. Have I? You're here to tell me she doesn't want a few bob?

PAT. Why shouldn't she? This is your child, this is the little girl you left at eleven because you couldn't be fagged looking after her. She's not going to get what she wanted then – love, care – a mother – we're thirty years too late with that one – money's all you've got isn't it, and she hasn't got any – yes I should think she does want a few bob.

VERA. Don't call *me*. No one barred you from tracking her down. You earn a decent living, I've seen you in the paper meeting Prince frigging Philip – you could have helped her yourself, but you're like me.

PAT. That's right. I'm like you. I never had a father. I'm assuming her father wasn't my father. I only had you – brought up the Vera way, what could I know – housework

stinks and black bras don't show the dirt. What else – don't
be warm, don't be kind, look after number one, stuff any
other bugger who does different – you made me, you stupid
cow, and you ballsed up.

VERA. Did I? Did I? Would you have got out if I hadn't shoved
you out? You want to be warm, you want to be kind, fine –
you end up slopping gravy about for eighty quid a week. You
should be thanking me for making you hard inside, because
that's what's pushed you on, that's what's kept you going –
there's a million bloody actresses out there, aren't there?
Paying her? You should be paying me.

MARGARET. I don't want anything.

*The removal men pass them and go down the stairs with a china
panther each.*

VERA. 'Course you do. But we don't all get what we want. I
did my share, two kids in a rotten council house, nosy
neighbours, useless bloody husband smoking himself to death.
What does it all matter now? We're just three middle-aged
women getting through this sod of a life.

There's a flash of a camera, and the three women are caught by
STELLA *and* BILLY *at the bottom of the stairs.*

STELLA. Oh that will be a nice one. Vera could we have you
with the panthers?

VERA. You can have me in a hammock with an Instant Whip,
you're paying. Would you excuse me, I must have a word
with the bailiffs.

VERA *leaves.* PAT *realises she's been done over and the fight goes
out of her. It takes* MARGARET *longer to catch up. They sit
down on a set of fancy dining-chairs outside the front door.*

PAT. The note from the fan.

STELLA. But I'm a huge fan, darling.

PAT. How much have you paid her?

STELLA. Only five. Not enough to leave the country which is

what she really wants. You wouldn't believe how many lives she's ruined.

PAT. Wouldn't we?

PAT *and* MARGARET *exchange a smile.*

STELLA. So your jigsaw's shaping up very nicely, Pat. Vera's jail sentence, your nude modelling.

PAT. Oh come on, that was a fashion shot.

STELLA. And of course your baby. (*Pause.*) It's very easy to trace an adoption these days you know.

PAT. Oh I know. He traced me. He's a trainee physiotherapist in Winnipeg. That's not such a good headline for you, is it? 'Pat Bedford's secret baby is a Canadian.'

STELLA. No, they're very bad news, the old Canadians.

PAT. Still, you've got plenty to send me down the tubes without him.

MARGARET (*standing up as her chair is removed by one of the men*). This is really unfair, this. What's Pat ever done? Had a father who died, had a mother who didn't know the meaning of the word. 'Cos really, Mum, she were crap. Sorry – but – she had a baby at fifteen, that's an accident, there's no shame, and he's fine – physiotherapy thingy – then she only goes on to become one of the biggest actresses on American television – what has she done wrong? You haven't, have you our Pat?

PAT. You tell the network. They're the ones who'll panic. How many *Peyton Places* did Mia Farrow do after she ran off with Frank Sinatra? She's had to adopt twelve Vietnamese orphans just to earn a living.

MARGARET (*to* STELLA). Well I don't know how you can live with yourself.

STELLA. I don't produce the dog poo darling, I just try to stop people planting geraniums in it. Though you're right in a way Margaret, it is a marvellous story. Wouldn't take too much to make you almost sympathetic, Pat.

PAT. And you'd do that, would you Stella?

STELLA. Well I might. You tell me everything. Margaret tells me everything.

MARGARET. Me?

STELLA. We've got it all then, you see. This is Roseanne Barr with knobs on.

PAT *still hasn't caught on.*

MARGARET. Opray Winfrey. Janet Jackson.

PAT. God I'm thick.

STELLA. We've got abuse, neglect, prostitution, missing sisters, lost babies, rags to riches. We're talking twelve weeks at number one here, film rights, mini-series . . .

PAT. Who'd play Margaret?

MARGARET. Meryl Streep.

PAT. What about Vera though?

STELLA. We'd have to tie her down to an exclusive. Otherwise she's a bit of a loose hypodermic.

VERA *strolls over to join them.*

VERA. Sorry to be so long. I was defrosting some kidneys.

PAT. Anyone we know?

MARGARET. Mum – did you ever love us?

VERA. I don't think so. I don't think I knew what love was till I bred my first Afghan.

STELLA. You see, what we really need is a happy ending.

VERA. Funnily enough, that's just what I was going to talk to my daughter about.

PAT *and* MARGARET *look at each other, unsure which daughter she means.*

The kitchens of the Kirkby Preston Services, later that day. PAT is giving away signed photographs and being very charming. MARGARET approaches BELLA tentatively.

MARGARET. I never said the job was rubbish. I love the job.

BELLA. Look – I am up to here in the wrong – I am just one big arsehole at times – everything in the papers were wrong – job's here if you want it.

MARGARET. I don't know. Can I take a week of my holidays – sort myself out?

SPOTTY BOY (*panicking behind the counter*). Bella – we're out of chips.

BELLA. Keep your acne on, terminator. Have a fabulous week, you deserve it.

MARGARET. Jim's not around is he?

BELLA. Not turned up. That Syreeta's hopping mad 'cos she's had to mop the urinals.

MARGARET waves her arm and leaves.

Outside JIM's house, the same afternoon. A miserable JIM is removing the name-strip from inside his windscreen, while MUM dusts the front gate. PAT's limo pulls up and MARGARET gets out.

MARGARET. Jim? Do you want to make it up or not?

MUM. Now, just a minute –

MARGARET. No conferring. If we're doing it, then we have to get a place, live together, none of this fannying about. We either go for it or it's finito.

MUM. There'll be no living together if I have anything to do with it.

JIM. You don't have anything to do with it, so button up or ship out – it's your fault they never learned me to read and I could never get a qualification. Yes – you're on, Margaret – I've loved you from the first minute you gave me extra gravy –

you've given me care and comfort and a wonderful sex life. Come here.

They embrace.

MUM. A sex life? You've had a sex life? Where have you had it?

JIM *stops kissing* MARGARET *long enough to answer.*

JIM. On your bed.

MUM. Not on the eiderdown.

Heathrow Airport, a few days later. PAT's *car is parked, and she is directing operations as a sweating* PORTER *loads her baggage on to a trolley, watched by* CLAIRE *and* MARGARET. PAT *is on a mobile phone.*

PAT. I beg your pardon? You can't promise to deliver them by Friday? In that case I can't promise to wear them for the Oscars, pose in them for *Vogue* magazine, or indeed patronise your tacky little third-rate operation on any future occasion. Good morning.

PORTER. Bloody hell.

PAT. Yes, that's the heavy one. Claire, you check the bags in, I'll meet you in the VIP lounge, with . . .

CLAIRE. Right you are.

PAT. I can't believe I'm doing this.

CLAIRE. Well, I think it's a brilliant wheeze, jolly well done you.

PAT. I wish Margaret would change her mind.

CLAIRE. Would make the whole thing jollier, wouldn't it?

PAT. Oh, here.

She hands over a bag with a baby's cardigan in it. CLAIRE *hugs her, remembers to give her her handbag.*

CLAIRE. Safe journey.

PAT. You too. Come on.

She hustles MARGARET *through the doors.*

You could still come, you know – I book an extra seat for the make-up.

MARGARET *laughs.*

MARGARET. I know there's nowt doing here, but what can we do, we have to give it a go.

PAT. I just quite fancied spending some time with somebody who didn't think the sun shone out of my backside.

MARGARET. Oh no, so it doesn't.

PAT. Well I'll need you to visit.

MARGARET. You blooming well will.

PAT. Bye.

They manage a clumsy hug.

Hang on. (*She pulls out a set of keys and an envelope from her bag.*)

MARGARET. What are them?

PAT. It says in the letter – I'll see you.

She hurries off. Heads turn and look at her. A WOMAN *near* MARGARET *stares at* PAT.

WOMAN. That's her off *Dynasty* – Stephanie Beacham.

MARGARET. Shut your mouth till you're less ignorant. (*She marches off, very pleased with herself.*)

The VIP lounge, a little later. PAT *is trying to relax with a magazine. A* STEWARDESS *bends over her. A woman next to her is reading a newspaper.*

STEWARDESS. Champagne, Miss Bedford? Mrs . . . ?

VERA *puts down her paper and takes a drink.*

VERA. Just call me Vera. Cheers! (*She looks over at* PAT's *magazine.*) Who's that then?

PAT. That's Jackie Stallone, Sylvester's mother. And that's Liz Taylor's mother. They're very big at the moment, celebrities' moms.

VERA. Oh, are they?

PAT *winces as she realises what she's said.*

The Swiss Cottage Café, a few nights later. Through the window we can see the café is closed and the chairs are on the tables. JIM *is mopping the floor and* MARGARET *happily polishes the red neon 'Café' sign. The camera swoops away from their little lighted haven into the night sky as we . . .*

. . . fade to black.

Lightning Source UK Ltd.
Milton Keynes UK
UKOW04f0429080118
315720UK00001B/9/P